DE WAA
Braai
buddy

bigger and better!

This book is dedicated to The Father, Son and Counsellor; my dear wife of 25 years, Eveline; my children Michelle and Samantha; Lynn and Paul Harvey; Chef Gino Polio; Myrna Robins; Colin Daniel; Carol and Ronnie Clift; my friends who frequent The Foresters Arms (Forries, still the best pub around); and all those who bought my first book.

ACKNOWLEDGEMENTS

I drew inspiration from the following books: *World Wide Cookbook* (published by Marshall Cavendish); *The Good Housekeeping Step-By-Step Cookbook* (published by Ebury, London); *The New Larousse Gastronomique*; *Ma Cuisine* (author: Auguste Escoffier); *Cooking the Portuguese Way in South Africa* (author: Mimi Jardim); *Woman's World 40th Birthday Celebration Cookbook*; *The South African All Colour Meat Cookbook* (author: Sannie Smit, published by Struik Publishers) and *The Complete South African Book of Food and Cookery* (authors: Sannie Smit and Margaret Fulton, published by Struik Publishers)

And the following magazines and newspapers, which over the last 30 years have provided me with more than just 'food for thought': *Cosmopolitan, Style, You, Personality, The Cape Argus, The Cape Times*.

First published in 2003 by Struik Publishers
(a division of New Holland Publishing
(South Africa) (Pty) Ltd)
Cornelis Struik House
80 McKenzie Street
Cape Town 8001

www.struik.co.za

New Holland Publishing is a member of Johnnic Communications Ltd

Copyright © in published edition: Struik Publishers 2003
Copyright © in text: De Waal Davis 2003
Copyright © in illustrations: Colin Daniel 2003

Reproduction by Hirt & Carter Cape (Pty) Ltd
Printed and bound by Paarl Print, Oosterland Street, Paarl, South Africa

All rights reserved. No part of this publication may be reproduced, stored in a retrieval system or transmitted, in any form or by any means, electronic, mechanical, photocopying, recording or otherwise, without the prior written permission of the copyright owner/s.

10 9 8 7 6 5 4 3

Publishing Manager: Linda de Villiers
Editor: Joy Clack
Designer: Beverley Dodd
Illustrator: Colin Daniel

Log on to our photographic website
www.imagesofafrica.co.za
for an African experience

ISBN 1 86872 880 3

Note: All measures are taken level.

1 tsp = 5 ml
1 Tbsp = 15 ml
1 cup = 250 ml

CONTENTS

Introduction	4	Burgers	46
Before you start	5	Kebabs	52
Know your meat	6	Sausages	60
The fire	7	Potjiekos	64
Marinades	8	Fish and seafood	78
Dry rubs	24	Favourite recipes	82
Bastes	28	Skottel cooking	88
Glazes	32	Spit-roasting	92
Sauces	36	Recipe index	95

INTRODUCTION

This *Braai Buddy* was originally compiled for close friends and relatives as a Christmas gift. Most of them, being South African, have ample experience in braaiing, so I have omitted cooking and grilling instructions when elementary. I have also tried to avoid compiling just another recipe book, and have instead attempted to give you something that will relieve the boredom of braaiing the same old 'chops and wors', and at the same time motivate your creative potential. Please do not make the mistake of looking at the ingredients of a particular recipe and then deciding if you are going to enjoy it or not. As in chemistry, where different formulas create different compounds, cooking different combinations of herbs and spices create completely different flavours. No single spice or herb should stand out alone, unless you are making a peri-peri dish or something similar. The combinations listed in the mix and match tables are merely suggestions and definitely not hard and fast rules.

So have fun!

This book is not for the serious chef, but is definitely for the serious braaier. The recipes are to be taken seriously, but for the rest, without prejudice, my tongue was so far in my cheek, it was sticking out of my ear!

De Waal Davis, March 2003

BEFORE YOU START ...

... make sure you have these ingredients in your cupboard.

The following spices, herbs and condiments are required for most of the marinades, bastes, glazes and sauces in this book. It is not suggested that you rush out and buy everything on this list, although these items are usually found in any well-stocked kitchen. Some of the herbs listed here are of the dried, bottled variety for convenience, but remember that, unless otherwise stated, fresh herbs are always better.

black pepper	dry red wine	mustard powder
brown sugar	dry white wine	olive oil
butter or margarine	fresh coriander leaves	paprika
chilli powder	fresh green chillies	salt or sea salt
chilli sauce	fresh parsley	soy sauce
chutney	fresh tarragon	sunflower oil
coriander seeds	fresh whole garlic	Tabasco sauce
cornflour (Maizena)	cloves	tomato paste
cumin seeds	grape vinegar	tomato sauce
dried basil	grated nutmeg	turmeric
dried mint	ground allspice	white pepper
dried origanum	ground ginger	white sugar
dried rosemary	honey	whole cloves
dried thyme	meat and fish masala	wine vinegar

KNOW YOUR MEAT

GRADING OF MEAT

The following are the grading specifications used by South African abattoirs and butcheries:

beef, lamb and mutton

TENDERNESS	CLASS	COLOUR
Most tender	A	Purple
Tender	AB	Green
Less tender	B	Brown
Least tender	C*	Red

FAT	CLASS
No fat	0*
Very lean	1
Lean	2
Medium	3*
Fat	4*
Over-fat	5*
Excessive fat	6*

Recommended grades: A1, A2, AB1 and AB2 (B1 and B2 are acceptable for beef if well matured).

* Not suitable for braaiing.

pork

% MEAT	FAT	CLASS	COLOUR
70+	< 12 mm	P	Purple
68–69	13–17 mm	O	Purple
66–67	18–22 mm	R*	Purple
64–65	23–27 mm	C*	Purple
62–63	28–32 mm	U*	Purple
< 61	32 mm+	S*	Purple

* Not suitable for braaiing.

BUYING FRESH MEAT

Beef: The colour of beef should be cherry red and the fat should be creamy white. Dark red or plum-coloured beef with yellow fat is usually an indication of an old animal.

Lamb and mutton: Lamb should be bright pink in colour and the fat should be white. Mutton should be slightly darker and the fat, as with lamb, should be white.

Pork: The colour of pork should be light pink and the fat should be white.

Braai buddy

MATURING FRESH MEAT

- Only mature whole or large cuts of meat. Small or thin cuts tend to dry out too quickly.
- Do not remove any fat from the meat as this will cause it to dry out. The fat may be removed when the maturing process is complete.
- Wipe the meat with vinegar or lemon juice to prevent bacteria from spoiling the meat.
- Do not mature pork or meat that has been frozen, sealed or vacuum-packed.
- Place the meat on a wire rack in the fridge, with a drip tray underneath. Air must be allowed to circulate at all times.
- The meat will lose mass due to loss of moisture.
- The edges of the meat might become dark and discoloured. This is normal and the dark pieces can be trimmed once maturation is complete.
- Beef can be matured for 5–10 days, mutton for 5–7 days and lamb for 2–5 days.

THE FIRE

Port Jackson — PROS: Use when nothing else available. CONS: Heat retention poor.

Rooikrans — PROS: Heat retention and aroma good, reduces to coals quickly, readily available. CONS: None.

Vine sticks — PROS: Heat retention and aroma very good, only available in Western Cape. CONS: Takes time to reduce to coals.

Camel thorn — PROS: Heat retention very good, aroma good, readily available in Namibia and Western Cape. CONS: None.

Mopane — PROS: Heat retention very good, aroma good, available in Lowveld. CONS: None.

Lead wood and bushwillow — PROS: Heat retention excellent, aroma very good, readily available in Lowveld. CONS: None.

Charcoal — PROS: Heat retention good, reduces to coals quickly, aroma neutral to good, readily available. CONS: Dirty to handle.

Briquettes — PROS: Heat retention excellent, available everywhere, can be doused with water and reused. CONS: Dirty to handle, aroma poor, takes longer to reduce to coals.

TESTING THE HEAT OF THE FIRE

This can roughly be tested by holding your open hand, palm side down, about 15–20 cm above the coals. Count the number of seconds before you have to pull your hand away.

Cool:	6–8 seconds
Medium:	4–6 seconds
Hot:	3–4 seconds
F.H.:	2–3 seconds

MARINADES

Marinades are used to moisten and to impart a particular flavour into the meat. The difference between marinades, bastes and sauces: marinades go **into** the meat, bastes go **onto** the meat, and sauces go **with** the meat.

TIPS AND HINTS

- Remove the marinated meat from the fridge the night before cooking (meat or fish should be at room temperature before braaiing).
- Whether or not acid-based marinades actually tenderize the meat is a contentious issue among cooks and chefs. To be on the safe side, always buy the best and most tender cut of meat that you can afford.
- Certain ingredients, such as pineapple, papaw, papinos, buttermilk and yoghurt, contain enzymes that definitely do break down the cellular structure of the meat, thus tenderizing it slightly, but once again always buy the best grades to ensure tenderness.
- Oil is used in a marinade mainly to moisten dry cuts of meat such as fillet, steak or pork fillet. When using fatty cuts of meat it is an unnecessary ingredient.
- Allow most of the marinade to drip off the meat before placing on the grid, as those with a high oil content will flame if braaiing over very hot coals.
- When marinating chicken, use a skewer to pierce the flesh in several places to enable the flavour to penetrate. Skinning the chicken will improve penetration.

- Some cooks suggest heating marinade and using it as a sauce when the cooking is completed. This should only be done when the oil content of the marinade is minimal, otherwise have plenty of toilet paper and a vacant toilet on hand. If you use the marinade as a sauce, remember to bring it to the boil first.
- If you want to tenderize large cuts of red meat, including game, without imparting any flavour into the meat, buttermilk, yoghurt, papaw or papaw leaves can be used. Soak the meat in one of the above or wrap in the leaves for 3 days. Wipe all the buttermilk, yoghurt or papaw off the meat using paper towels, then season or baste with Basic basting mix (page 30) mixed with fresh lemon juice.
- Most marinades are uncooked and should not be used as sauces, unless instructed otherwise.
- Larger cuts, such as roasts, legs, shoulders and flank, should be marinated for three days, turning every 12 hours and kept refrigerated during the process. These cuts should be fully immersed in the marinade.
- Tender cuts can be marinated for 2–4 hours, turning often to ensure a uniform coating.
- For best results, fully immerse meat, poultry or fish in marinade, rather than just coating it.
- Marinade ingredients can be mixed or combined in the following ways: blended in a food processor, shaken vigorously in a bottle or beaten with a whisk or an eggbeater.
- When marinating large cuts of meat, simply use a plastic shopping or carrier bag if you don't have a large enough bowl. Place the meat and marinade in the bag, tie the handles into a knot, shake and refrigerate.

MIX AND MATCH

The numbers in the table overleaf are recipe numbers, not page numbers. The table represents the most common cuts of meat, poultry and fish that you would use in preparing a braai menu. In the list of meats, I have included terminology common to Western, European and Mediterranean cuisine. Several different names might be used for the same cut of meat, for example sirloin might be known as strip loin, porterhouse, entrecôte, minute steak, escallops, and so on; rump might be known as club steak, club rump, lazy aged steak, old man's steak, and so on; fillet might be known as fillet mignon, tournedos, medallions, Chateaubriand, and so on. This is purely to assist you in communicating with your butcher or when using other cookbooks.

The table also represents the many variations of marinades that can be used with the same cut of meat, poultry or fish. Simply choose your meat from the meat section and match it with a marinade in the suggested marinades section.

Most marinades can be used as bastes, except No. 16 (Yoghurt or buttermilk marinade).

There is no hard and fast rule regarding which combination of meat/marinade to use. The red wine with red meat, and white wine with chicken and fish rule should be thrown out the window. How can someone else tell you what you should enjoy?

The table overleaf is a 'kick start' for your creative potential, and also demonstrates some of the many combinations that may be used.

Always use a plastic or glass container in which to marinade your meat.

Marinades

BEEF

Steaks
Fillet (5 cm thick), Rump (2.5 cm thick), T-bone (2.5 cm thick), Sirloin (3 cm thick), Porterhouse (2.5 cm thick), Tournedos (2.5 cm thick), Chateaubriand (5–8 cm thick), Minute (1 cm thick)
SUGGESTED MARINADES:
Nos 4, 6, 8, 9, 10, 11, 23, 32, 36, 42
MARINATING TIME: 2–4 hours

Kebabs
SUGGESTED MARINADES:
Nos 4, 8, 9, 11, 14, 18, 23, 32, 33, 36
MARINATING TIME: 4–6 hours

Whole cuts
Aitchbone, Flat rib, Fore rib, Prime rib, Rib-eye, Scotch fillet, Thick rib, Topside, Wing rib
SUGGESTED MARINADES:
Nos 4, 6, 7, 8, 9, 10, 11, 15, 16, 21, 22, 23, 32, 36, 42, 43, 48, 49
MARINATING TIME: 2–3 days

LAMB

Chops
Loin, Chump, Best end of neck, Saddle, Shoulder, Cutlets
SUGGESTED MARINADES:
Nos 1, 6, 8, 11, 13, 14, 21, 31, 32, 33, 34, 36, 37, 38, 40, 44, 45, 49
MARINATING TIME: 2–4 hours

Kebabs
SUGGESTED MARINADES:
Nos 4, 8, 11, 12, 13, 14, 21, 30, 31, 32, 33, 34, 38, 44
MARINATING TIME: 4 hours+

Whole spit-roast
See chapter on spit-roasting (page 92)

Whole cuts
Butterflied leg
SUGGESTED MARINADES:
Nos 1, 6, 8, 13, 14, 16, 21, 34, 36, 37, 38
MARINATING TIME: 2–3 days

Shoulder, Loin, Rolled loin, Ribs, Breast, Flank, Saddle, Rack
SUGGESTED MARINADES:
Nos 1, 6, 8, 13, 14, 21, 34, 36, 37, 38
MARINATING TIME: 2–3 days

PORK – FRESH, UNSMOKED

Chops, steaks and ribs
Loin, Neck, Cutlets, Escallops, Neck steaks, Leg steaks, Fillet, Ribs, Riblets
SUGGESTED MARINADES:
Nos 4, 5, 8, 9, 18, 20, 21, 22, 23, 30, 32, 37, 39, 46, 47
MARINATING TIME: 2–4 hours

Kebabs
SUGGESTED MARINADES:
Nos 4, 5, 8, 9, 11, 12, 18, 20, 21, 22, 23, 30, 32, 33, 37, 39, 41, 46, 47, 48
MARINATING TIME: 4 hours+

Whole cuts
Rib, Loin, Saddle, Neck (deboned), Neck (on the bone), Fresh eisbein, Hock or shank, Belly, Rolled belly
SUGGESTED MARINADES:
Nos 4, 8, 9, 20, 21, 23, 32, 37, 39, 41, 46
MARINATING TIME: 24 hours

Whole spit-roast
See chapter on spit-roasting (page 92)

Braai buddy

PORK –
SMOKED, CURED

Chops
Kassler, Bacon, Neck, Gammon steaks, Neck steaks
SUGGESTED MARINADES:
None, see bastes (page 29) and glazes (page 33)

Whole cuts
Gammon, Spare rib, Loin, Neck
SUGGESTED MARINADES:
None, see bastes (page 29) and glazes (page 33)

POULTRY

Baby chicken, Spring chicken, Turkey, Broiler
SUGGESTED MARINADES:
Nos 1, 2, 3, 4, 5, 8, 9, 17, 18, 19, 20, 21, 22, 23, 25, 28, 29, 32, 39, 48
MARINATING TIME: 4–24 hours

Kebabs
SUGGESTED MARINADES:
Nos 1, 2, 3, 4, 5, 8, 9, 17, 18, 19, 20, 21, 22, 23, 25, 28, 29, 32, 39, 48
MARINATING TIME: 4–6 hours

SEAFOOD

Line fish, Gamefish, Trawled fish
SUGGESTED MARINADES:
Nos 17, 19, 25, 27, 28, 29
MARINATING TIME: 1–2 hours

Shellfish
Prawns, Crayfish
SUGGESTED MARINADES:
None, see bastes (page 29)

Calamari
SUGGESTED MARINADES:
Nos 28, 29
MARINATING TIME: 3–4 hours

Kebabs
SUGGESTED MARINADES:
Nos 17, 19, 21, 23, 25, 27, 28, 29
MARINATING TIME: 1–2 hours

Marinades

When concocting your own marinade, the usual ratio between oil and all the other ingredients (vinegar, wine, tomato sauce, etc.) should be 1:5.

1. Greek-style

½ cup olive oil
1 cup dry white wine
1 cup fresh lemon juice
½ cup water
6 cloves garlic, crushed
a few sprigs fresh rosemary or origanum (not both)

Can be used as a marinade and baste for lamb, pork or poultry.

Makes 3 cups

2. Peri-peri

1 cup olive oil
½ cup chopped fresh chillies*
½ cup dry white wine
2 Tbsp coarse salt
10 cloves garlic, crushed
2 Tbsp dried origanum
3 Tbsp fresh lemon juice
2 tsp sugar

Can be used as a marinade and baste for poultry or seafood.

Makes 2½ cups

* For those with sensitive palates, remove seeds by splitting the chilli lengthways and scooping them out with a teaspoon.

3. Tandoori

1½ tsp paprika
½ cup plain yoghurt
1 Tbsp sunflower oil
2 tsp fresh lemon juice
2 cloves garlic, crushed
1 tsp ground ginger
1½ tsp ground coriander
1½ tsp ground cumin
1 tsp salt
orange or red food colouring

BAGHAAR (spicy sauce to prevent the cooked meat from drying out)

5 Tbsp butter
3 Tbsp sunflower oil, heated
1 dried red chilli
1 clove garlic, crushed
½ tsp cumin seeds
½ tsp onion or mustard seeds

Mix all the marinade ingredients together and marinate the meat for 8 hours before braaiing. For the baghaar, heat the butter and oil in a pan and fry all the remaining ingredients until browned. Spoon the baghaar over the chicken after braaiing, or just before serving, to prevent the meat from drying out.

Makes enough for 1 chicken

Braai buddy

4. Lemon and tarragon

6 Tbsp fresh lemon juice
4 tsp sunflower oil
2 small onions, finely chopped
4 Tbsp chopped fresh tarragon
4 tsp French mustard
2 cloves garlic, crushed
salt and freshly ground black pepper

Can be used as a marinade and baste for pork, lamb, poultry or seafood.

Makes 2/3 cup

5. Honey

4 Tbsp fresh lemon juice
3/4 cup soy sauce
6 Tbsp honey
5 cloves garlic, crushed
3/4 cup chopped fresh parsley

Can be used as a marinade and baste for pork or poultry.

Makes 1 cup

6. Red wine

1 cup dry red wine
1 tsp dried basil or origanum
2 cloves garlic, crushed
1 onion, chopped
1 carrot, chopped
1 stick table celery, chopped
1 bay leaf
10 black peppercorns
2 Tbsp brown vinegar
2 Tbsp sunflower oil
1 tsp salt

Can be used as a marinade for beef, game or lamb.

Makes 1½ cups

7. Beer

1 x 340 ml can beer
1 onion, finely chopped
2½ Tbsp sunflower oil
2 Tbsp soy sauce
1 Tbsp brown sugar
1 Tbsp finely chopped fresh root ginger
salt and freshly ground black pepper

Can be used as a marinade and baste for beef, pork and poultry.

Makes 1 2/3 cups

Beer or wine left in the sun for more than 30 seconds will spoil.

Marinades

8. Caribbean

1 red pepper, finely chopped
1 onion, finely chopped
1 chilli, finely chopped
2 Tbsp grated fresh root ginger
2 Tbsp chopped fresh parsley
1 Tbsp snipped fresh chives
3 Tbsp soy sauce
3 Tbsp olive oil
grated rind and juice of 1 lime
2 Tbsp raisins
2 Tbsp soft brown sugar

Can be used as a marinade and baste for pork, veal or poultry.

Makes 1 cup

9. Teriyaki

3 Tbsp honey or brown sugar
3 Tbsp sunflower oil
½ cup soy sauce
2 Tbsp dry red wine
2 tsp grated fresh root ginger
3 cloves garlic, crushed

Use for cubed beef (rump) on a skewer and interspersed with pineapple cubes. Chicken and pork may also be used.

Makes 1 cup

10. Cola

1 x 375 ml can cola
5 Tbsp sunflower oil
juice of ½ lemon
½ tsp ground ginger (optional)

Can be used as a marinade and baste for beef.

Makes 1⅔ cups

11. Basic BBQ

1 cup dry sherry
¾ cup soy sauce
1 cup sunflower oil
½ cup Worcestershire sauce
4 cloves garlic, crushed
freshly ground black pepper

Can be used as a marinade or baste for beef, poultry, pork, veal and fish.

Makes 3 cups

12. For sosaties

2–3 large onions, sliced
3 cloves garlic, crushed
2 Tbsp sunflower oil
2 Tbsp medium curry powder
1 small chilli
3 bay leaves
3 tsp chopped fresh root ginger
2 Tbsp smooth apricot jam
1⅓ cups red wine vinegar
2 cups milk

Fry the onions and garlic in the oil, add curry powder and fry for 2 minutes. Add remaining ingredients, except milk, and simmer for 10 minutes. Remove from the heat, add milk, then cool. Marinate lamb or pork for 24 hours before threading onto skewers.

Makes 4–5 cups

13. For shish kebabs

1¼ cups tomato juice
1 tsp mustard powder
½ cup plain yoghurt
¼ tsp ground cinnamon
½ tsp salt
¼ tsp freshly ground black pepper

Marinate cubes of lamb or beef for 24 hours before threading onto skewers.

Makes 1¾ cups

14. Moroccan

4 small onions, finely chopped
2 tsp salt
4 tsp ground ginger
2 tsp freshly ground black pepper
4 tsp ground cumin
¾ cup olive oil
4 tsp paprika
a pinch of cayenne pepper or
  a dash of Tabasco sauce

Use with thinly sliced lamb, beef or chicken. Drain well, then stir-fry.

Makes 1 cup

15. Kidney and liver

⅔ cup olive oil
6 Tbsp dry red wine
2 tsp dried thyme
salt and freshly ground black pepper

Use for Lamb's kidney and liver kebabs (page 56).

Makes 1¼ cups

Marinades

16. Yoghurt or buttermilk

4 cups Bulgarian yoghurt or buttermilk

Some or all of the following herbs may be used, but for a neutral flavour, use yoghurt or buttermilk only, which will tenderize the meat without changing the flavour.

10 tsp chopped fresh mint
10 tsp chopped fresh origanum
10 tsp chopped fresh rosemary
2 cloves garlic, crushed
1 tsp ground cumin

Marinate for 3 days, turning meat every 12 hours. Keep refrigerated. Remove all the marinade using paper towel **before braaiing**, then use a recommended baste as listed in the table on page 29.

Makes 4 cups

17. For seafood

½ cup dry white wine
3 Tbsp sunflower oil
1 tsp paprika
½ tsp salt
a pinch of white pepper
1 tsp sugar
¾ Tbsp chopped fresh parsley

Makes ¾ cup

18. For satay (Indonesian)

¾ Tbsp salt
1 medium onion, chopped
1 Tbsp ground coriander
½ tsp freshly ground black pepper
3 Tbsp fresh lemon juice
6 Tbsp soy sauce
6 Tbsp peanut butter
6 Tbsp sunflower oil
4 Tbsp brown sugar
2 cloves garlic, crushed
a dash of Tabasco sauce

Can be used as a marinade and baste for veal, pork, chicken or kebabs.

Makes 1⅔ cups

19. For fish

2 Tbsp olive oil
2 Tbsp sunflower oil or melted butter
2 Tbsp fresh lemon juice
½ cup dry white wine
4 chillies, seeded and chopped
2 cloves garlic, chopped
2 spring onions, white part only, chopped
a pinch of sugar

Combine all the ingredients and pour over the fish. Can also be used for shellfish.

Makes ¾ cup

20. For chicken (savoury)

10 cloves garlic, crushed
¾ cup tarragon vinegar
2 Tbsp sugar
2 Tbsp sunflower oil
2 Tbsp Worcestershire sauce
1 Tbsp mustard powder
1 tsp salt

Can also be used for fish and pork.

Makes 1 cup

21. Lime

⅔ cup fresh lime juice
4 Tbsp sunflower oil
1½ Tbsp lime zest
1 tsp salt
½ tsp crushed black peppercorns

Can be used as a marinade and baste for chicken, pork, lamb and fish.

Makes ¾ cup

22. Orange and herb

⅔ cup dry white wine
3 Tbsp olive oil
juice of 2 oranges
1 tsp chopped fresh rosemary
1 tsp chopped fresh thyme
1 tsp chopped fresh marjoram or origanum
1 clove garlic, crushed

Can be used as a marinade and baste for chicken and pork.

Makes ¾ cup

23. Spring onion and soy

⅔ cup soy sauce
3 Tbsp dry sherry
6 Tbsp finely sliced spring onion
3 Tbsp brown sugar
½ tsp salt
½ tsp ground ginger

Can be used for chicken, pork and fish.

Makes 1½ cups

When marinating chicken, pierce it all over with a skewer to enable the marinade to penetrate.

Marinades

24. For fajitas

1 cup fresh orange juice
½ cup sunflower oil
4 Tbsp dry red wine
4 Tbsp fresh lemon juice
½ tsp cayenne pepper
½ tsp freshly ground black pepper
¼ tsp ground cumin
2 cloves garlic, crushed

Makes 1¾ cups

25. For Portuguese swordfish

⅓ cup olive oil
2 tsp finely chopped garlic
1 Tbsp fresh lemon juice
1 tsp chopped fresh parsley
1 tsp chopped fresh thyme
salt and freshly ground black pepper
½ cup dry white wine
2 Tbsp dry sherry

Makes ¾ cup

26. Peri-peri oil

3 Tbsp chopped dried Portuguese chillies, with seeds
1½ cups olive oil
2 cloves garlic, crushed
3 Tbsp fresh lemon juice
½ tsp salt
½ tsp freshly ground black pepper
2 Tbsp whisky

Substitute 375 g butter, melted for olive oil if using as a sauce.

Makes 1¾ cups

27. Fish masala

3 Tbsp sunflower oil
1 tsp ground coriander
1 tsp ground cumin
1 tsp turmeric
1 small chilli, finely chopped
1 clove garlic, crushed
1 onion, finely chopped
1 Tbsp fresh lemon juice
1 tomato, skinned, seeded and puréed
a pinch of freshly ground black pepper

Makes ⅔ cup

When a marinade is required but you don't have any ingredients, use a salad dressing that does not contain mayonnaise or eggs.

Braai buddy

28. For calamari (Italian)

6 Tbsp olive oil
6 Tbsp fresh lemon juice
salt and freshly ground black pepper
1 Tbsp chopped fresh origanum
2 Tbsp soy sauce

Combine all the ingredients and marinate the calamari for 3–4 hours. Remove calamari from marinade and grill or braai for 3–5 minutes, turning only once during cooking.

Makes enough for 500 g calamari

29. For calamari (Chinese)

1 tsp grated fresh root ginger
4 tsp sugar
4 tsp anchovy paste
½ cup fish stock

Combine all ingredients and marinate the calamari for 3–4 hours. Remove calamari from marinade and grill or braai for 3–5 minutes, turning only once during cooking.

Makes enough for 500 g calamari

30. Apple

2½ cups apple juice
½ tsp ground cinnamon
½ tsp chilli powder
1 Tbsp finely chopped onion
¼ tsp freshly ground black pepper
1 tsp salt

Can be used for pork or lamb.

Makes 2½ cups

31. Apricot and onion

½ cup canned apricots, drained
1 tsp Worcestershire sauce
1 Tbsp sunflower oil
1 Tbsp brown vinegar
2 Tbsp finely chopped onions, fried in oil
  until lightly browned
3 spring onions, finely sliced
1 Tbsp fresh lemon juice
½ tsp sugar

This marinade must be blended in a processor. Can be used for pork, lamb and chicken.

Makes ¾ cup

32. Mustard and herb

4 Tbsp olive oil
2 Tbsp dry red wine
2 tsp brown sugar
2 tsp prepared mild mustard
2 Tbsp finely chopped fresh mixed herbs
1 Tbsp finely chopped fresh parsley

Can be used for beef, lamb, pork, veal and chicken.

Makes ⅓ cup

33. Martini

2½ cups dry martini (vermouth)
4 Tbsp sunflower oil
2 Tbsp white vinegar
12 black peppercorns, crushed
1 bay leaf
½ tsp dried thyme
a sprig of fresh tarragon

Can be used for beef, lamb or pork.

Makes 3 cups

34. For Spanish kebabs

1½ cups tomato juice
¾ cup dry sherry
4 Tbsp fresh lemon juice
2 Tbsp sunflower oil
2 Tbsp brown vinegar
2 fresh green chillies, very finely chopped
1 red pepper, finely chopped
2 onions, finely chopped
4 cloves garlic, crushed
1 tsp dried origanum

Use for Spanish kebabs (page 58).

Makes 2½ cups

35. Yoghurt

1 cup plain yoghurt
1 Tbsp capers
2 Tbsp chopped spring onion
2 tsp French mustard
½ cup fresh orange juice
¼ tsp salt

Mix the marinade ingredients together, pour over prime rib roast and marinate for 4 hours. While the meat is roasting, baste frequently with the marinade.

Makes 1¾ cups

Braai buddy

36. For beef or lamb

1 cup dry red wine
4 Tbsp red wine vinegar
2 Tbsp olive oil
12 bay leaves

Makes 1⅓ cups

37. For pork or lamb

½ cup olive oil
2 Tbsp fresh lemon juice
coarse salt and freshly ground black pepper
2 cloves garlic, chopped
1 bay leaf
a sprig of fresh rosemary

Makes ⅔ cup

38. For lamb chops

½ cup olive oil
3 Tbsp fresh lemon juice
2 tsp finely chopped garlic
salt and freshly ground black pepper
¼ tsp ground cumin
2 Tbsp chopped fresh mint

Makes ¾ cup

39. For chicken or pork

½ cup olive oil
3 Tbsp fresh lemon juice
2 tsp finely chopped garlic
salt and freshly ground black pepper
2 Tbsp tomato purée
2 Tbsp soy sauce
1 tsp grated fresh root ginger
1 Tbsp chopped fresh coriander leaves

Makes 1 cup

40. For whole cuts of lamb (herb)

½ cup dry white wine
½ cup white wine vinegar
3 Tbsp sunflower oil
2 Tbsp prepared mustard
1 Tbsp Worcestershire sauce
1 small onion, chopped
½ tsp each dried rosemary and origanum
salt and freshly ground black pepper
4 Tbsp tomato paste

Makes 1½ cups

Marinades

41. For whole cuts of pork

4 Tbsp honey
4 Tbsp red wine vinegar
2 Tbsp brown sugar
4 Tbsp soy sauce
2 cloves garlic, crushed
1 cup beer
1 cup meat stock

Makes 2½ cups

42. For grilled beef flat rib

1 x 340 ml can beer
1 Tbsp honey
1 tsp soy sauce
2 tsp chopped fresh root ginger
2 Tbsp sunflower oil
1 clove garlic, crushed
3 spring onions, chopped
1 tsp prepared mustard
a sprig of fresh parsley

Makes 2½ cups

43. For butterflied shoulder of lamb

3 Tbsp sunflower oil
2 Tbsp brown sugar
1½ tsp ground ginger
⅓ cup chutney
3 Tbsp brown vinegar
⅔ cup preserved ginger, chopped

Makes 1½ cups

44. For Saratoga chops

1 clove garlic, crushed
2 Tbsp sunflower oil
2 tsp soy sauce
2 Tbsp red wine vinegar
1 bay leaf
½ tsp brown sugar
1 Tbsp tomato paste
3 Tbsp dry white wine or meat stock

Makes ½ cup

45. For steaks (soy and ginger)

½ cup sunflower oil
3 Tbsp soy sauce
3 cloves garlic, crushed
2 tsp ground ginger
½ tsp brown sugar
1 tsp mustard powder

Makes ½ cup

46. For pork chops

4 Tbsp soy sauce
½ cup dry sherry
2 Tbsp brown sugar
a small piece fresh root ginger, grated
1 clove garlic, crushed with ½ tsp salt

Makes 1 cup

47. Port

3 Tbsp port
2 Tbsp sunflower oil
3 Tbsp chopped onion
½ tsp salt
¼ tsp freshly ground black pepper

Use for pork chops, steaks or kebabs.

Makes ⅔ cup

48. Poultry herb mix

4 Tbsp bruised and chopped fresh basil
¾ cup bruised and chopped fresh parsley
⅓ cup bruised and chopped fresh thyme
4 Tbsp bruised and chopped fresh origanum
4 Tbsp bruised and chopped fresh sage
3 Tbsp chopped fresh rosemary
10 bay leaves, crumbled

Sprinkle a small handful of the mixed herbs over the hot coals before placing the poultry on the grill. During cooking, sprinkle more herbs over the coals at regular intervals.

Makes about 2 cups

49. Meat herb mix

¾ cup fresh parsley, bruised and chopped
½ cup fresh marjoram, bruised and chopped
½ cup fresh thyme, bruised and chopped
¾ cup fresh basil, bruised and chopped
3 Tbsp chopped fresh rosemary
4 Tbsp juniper berries
1 Tbsp black peppercorns
5 bay leaves, crumbled

Sprinkle a small handful of the mixed herbs over the hot coals before placing the meat on the grill. During cooking, sprinkle more herbs over the coals at regular intervals.

Makes about 2 cups

Marinades

DRY RUBS

Dry rubs are dry marinades or dry bastes. The ingredients are mixed thoroughly, then rubbed all over the meat, poultry or fish.

TIPS AND HINTS

- When cooking a large cut of meat or fish, first make diagonal slashes across it, then press the dry rub into the cuts and all over the meat or fish.
- Always use dried herbs for dry rubs.
- Store in an airtight container away from sunlight.

BEEF

Steaks
Fillet (4 cm thick), Rump (2.5 cm thick), T-bone (2.5 cm thick), Sirloin (3 cm thick), Porterhouse (2.5 cm thick), Tornedos (2.5 cm thick), Chateaubriand (5–8 cm thick), Minute (1 cm thick)
SUGGESTED RUBS: Nos 51, 53, 54
MARINATING TIME: 2–4 hours

Kebabs
SUGGESTED RUBS: None, see marinades (page 10)

Whole cuts
Aitchbone, Flat rib, Fore rib, Prime rib, Rib-eye, Scotch fillet, Thick rib, Topside, Wing rib
SUGGESTED RUBS: None, see marinades (page 10)

LAMB

Chops
Loin, Chump, Best end of neck, Saddle, Shoulder, Cutlets
SUGGESTED RUBS: Nos 51, 53
MARINATING TIME: 2–4 hours

Kebabs
SUGGESTED RUBS: None, see marinades (page 10)

Whole spit-roast
None, see bastes (page 29)

Whole cuts
Butterflied leg, Shoulder, Loin, Rolled loin, Ribs, Breast, Flank, Saddle, Rack
SUGGESTED RUBS: None, see marinades (page 10)

PORK –
FRESH, UNSMOKED

Chops
Loin, Neck, Cutlets, Escallops, Neck steaks, Leg steaks, Fillet, Ribs, Riblets
SUGGESTED RUBS: Nos 51, 53
MARINATING TIME: 2–4 hours

Kebabs
SUGGESTED RUBS: None, see marinades (page 10)

Whole cuts
Rib, Loin, Saddle, Neck (deboned), Neck (on the bone), Fresh eisbein, Hock or shank, Belly, Rolled belly
SUGGESTED RUBS: None, see marinades (page 10)

Whole spit-roast
SUGGESTED RUBS: None, see bastes (page 29)

PORK –
SMOKED, CURED

Chops and steaks
Kassler, Bacon, Neck, Gammon
SUGGESTED RUBS: None, see bastes (page 29)

Whole cuts
Gammon, Spare rib, Loin, Neck
SUGGESTED RUBS: None, see bastes (page 29)

POULTRY
Baby chicken, Spring chicken, Turkey, Broiler
SUGGESTED RUBS: Nos 51, 53
MARINATING TIME: 2–4 hours

Kebabs
SUGGESTED RUBS: None, see marinades (page 11)

SEAFOOD
Line fish, Gamefish, Trawled fish
SUGGESTED RUBS: Nos 50, 52
MARINATING TIME: 2–4 hours

Shellfish
SUGGESTED RUBS: None, see bastes (page 29)

Kebabs
SUGGESTED RUBS: None, see marinades (page 11)

Dry rubs

50. Tandoori mix

1 Tbsp paprika
1 Tbsp coriander seeds, ground
1 Tbsp cumin seeds, ground
1 Tbsp ground ginger
1 tsp turmeric

Can be used for seafood.

Makes 4 Tbsp

How to avoid a hangover!

1. Eat something or drink a glass of milk at least 30 minutes before drinking alcohol.
2. Don't mix your drinks. If you are a beer and wine drinker, drink your beer first, then change to wine. Never switch to beer after wine.
3. Smoke fewer cigarettes.
4. Drink at least 500 ml water before going to sleep. Vitamin C and B complex will help.
5. The morning after: Drink a glass of orange juice or milk. One hour later have a breakfast that includes eggs in any form whatsoever.
6. If all of the above fails, have another beer and try again tomorrow.

---

51. Cajun spice mix

1 Tbsp cayenne pepper
1 Tbsp white pepper
1 Tbsp freshly ground black pepper
1 Tbsp dried thyme
1 Tbsp dried origanum
1 Tbsp brown sugar
1 Tbsp paprika
1 Tbsp garlic powder

Combine all the ingredients. Roll or press the meat, chicken or fish into the mixture about 10 minutes before cooking. Once coated, place the meat, chicken or fish into a hot, dry, cast-iron frying pan and fry quickly on each side to 'blacken' (New Orleans-style) and seal in the juices. Then proceed to grill or fry as normal.

Makes ½ cup

52. Dry fish masala

1 Tbsp ground coriander
1 Tbsp ground cumin
1 Tbsp turmeric
1 tsp freshly ground black pepper
½ tsp chilli powder
½ Tbsp garlic powder

Makes 4 Tbsp

53. Basic dry rub

4 Tbsp mustard powder
2 tsp paprika
1 tsp garlic powder
1 tsp dried thyme

Can be used for beef, lamb, pork and chicken.

Makes about ⅓ cup

54. Dry marinade

6 bay leaves
½ tsp ground cloves
1 tsp grated nutmeg
1 tsp dried thyme
2 tsp paprika
1 tsp crushed dried chillies
¼ tsp ground allspice
½ tsp ground cinnamon
½ tsp dried basil
½ tsp dried origanum
¼ tsp freshly ground black pepper
2 tsp mustard powder

Process all the ingredients in a blender until fine. Can be used for steaks.

Makes 4–5 Tbsp

Never, ever, throw cigarette or cigar butts into the fire while cooking!

BASTES

Bastes are used to impart flavour onto the meat. Most bastes are uncooked and are normally used to coat tender cuts of meat that require only short cooking times. Remember that most marinades can be used as a baste, with the exception of No. 16 Yoghurt or buttermilk marinade.

TIPS AND HINTS

- When basting large cuts of meat that have not been marinated, such as whole rump or sirloin, only apply the baste during the last stages of cooking, to avoid burning.
- When a baste is required for spit-roasting or any other long-term grilling process, use No. 1 Greek-style marinade with ⅔ cup water added.

BEEF

Steaks
Fillet (4 cm thick), Rump (2.5 cm thick), T-bone (2.5 cm thick), Sirloin (3 cm thick), Porterhouse (2.5 cm thick), Tornedos (2.5 cm thick), Chateaubriand (5–8 cm thick), Minute (1 cm thick)
SUGGESTED BASTES: Nos 55, 58, 61

Kebabs
SUGGESTED BASTES: None, see marinades (page 10)

Whole cuts
Aitchbone, Flat rib, Fore rib, Prime rib, Rib-eye, Scotch fillet, Thick rib, Topside, Wing rib
SUGGESTED BASTES: None, see marinades (page 10)

LAMB

Chops
Loin, Chump, Best end of neck, Saddle, Shoulder, Cutlets
SUGGESTED BASTES: Nos 55, 56, 60, 62, 63

Kebabs
SUGGESTED BASTES: None, see marinades (page 10)

Whole spit-roast
SUGGESTED BASTES: Use marinade nos 1, 11, 21, 22

Whole cuts
Butterflied leg, Shoulder, Loin, Rolled loin, Ribs, Breast, Flank, Saddle, Rack
SUGGESTED BASTES: None, see marinades (page 10)

PORK — FRESH, UNSMOKED

Chops
Loin, Neck, Cutlets, Escallops, Neck steaks, Leg steaks, Fillet, Ribs, Riblets
SUGGESTED BASTES: Nos 55, 56, 57, 62

Kebabs
SUGGESTED BASTES: None, see marinades (page 10)

Whole cuts
Rib, Loin, Saddle, Neck (on the bone), Neck (deboned), eisbein, Hock/shank, Belly, Rolled belly
SUGGESTED BASTES: None, see marinades (page 10)

Whole spit-roast
SUGGESTED BASTES: Use marinade no. 1 (replace wine and lemon juice with apple juice)

PORK — SMOKED, CURED

Chops and steaks
Kassler, Bacon, Neck, Gammon
SUGGESTED BASTES: No. 58, see also glazes (page 33)

Whole cuts
Gammon, Spare rib, Loin, Neck
SUGGESTED BASTES: No. 58, see also glazes (page 33)

POULTRY
Baby chicken, Spring chicken, Turkey, Broiler
SUGGESTED BASTES: Nos 55, 57, 61, 62, 63

Kebabs
SUGGESTED BASTES: None, see marinades (page 11)

SEAFOOD
Line fish, Gamefish, Trawled fish
SUGGESTED BASTES: Nos 55, 57, 59, 62, 63

Shellfish
SUGGESTED BASTES: Nos 55, 57, 59, 62, 63 or garlic butter

Kebabs
SUGGESTED BASTES: None, see marinades (page 11)

Bastes

55. Basic mix

4 Tbsp mustard powder
1 tsp paprika
½ tsp salt
½ clove garlic, crushed and chopped
4 Tbsp sunflower oil
4 Tbsp melted butter

Mix all the ingredients together thoroughly, then brush the meat, chicken or fish before and during cooking. Four tablespoons of lemon juice may be added, but this will slow browning.

Makes ½ cup

56. Apple and chilli

1½ cups canned apple sauce
½ cup chilli sauce
2 cloves garlic, crushed
2 Tbsp brown sugar
1 Tbsp fresh lemon juice
2 Tbsp honey
1 Tbsp Worcestershire sauce
2 tsp chopped fresh rosemary
¼ tsp salt

Process all the ingredients in a blender until smooth, then spread over the meat. Braai over medium coals, turning occasionally. This baste can be used for pork or lamb.

Makes 2¼ cups

57. BBQ chicken

1 clove garlic, crushed
1 tsp mustard powder
1 tsp chilli powder
1 tsp paprika
1 Tbsp peach or apricot jam
1 Tbsp grated onion
2 Tbsp tomato sauce
1 Tbsp Worcestershire sauce
½ cup brown vinegar
½ cup sunflower oil

Combine all the ingredients, then brush over the chicken before cooking, and each time the chicken is turned. This baste can also be used for fish and pork.

Makes 1⅓ cups

58. Spare rib

1 x 470 g bottle chutney
1 cup brown vinegar
1 cup soft brown sugar

Place all the ingredients in a saucepan, bring to the boil and stir until the sugar dissolves. Allow to cool slightly, then turn to the Spare ribs recipe on page 84. This baste can also be used for steak and chicken, but only apply to the chicken during the last stages of cooking. It can also be used as a glaze or a sauce.

Makes 4 cups

Be careful when using marinades, bastes and glazes as they tend to burn if cooked for too long or over a high heat, especially if they contain sugar, chutney or tomato sauce.

Braai buddy

59. Portuguese red pepper paste

10–12 red peppers
1 cup coarse salt

Halve the peppers, remove the seeds and slit the peppers lengthways so that they lie completely flat. Place a layer of peppers in a bowl and sprinkle generously with the salt. Repeat the layers until you have used up all the peppers. Refrigerate. After a day or two a brine will form. Place a heavy object on top of the peppers so that they are immersed in the brine, then leave for another 5–6 days. Drain the peppers, rinse lightly and place them on a wire rack to drain. Pat dry, then blend the peppers into a paste. Spoon the paste into sterilized jars, leaving a gap at the top. Fill this gap with olive oil, then seal the jars and store in the fridge. A few cloves of garlic and a little olive oil may also be added during the blending process.
Can be used for seafood.

Makes about 6 cups

60. For roast beef

3 Tbsp dry red wine
3 Tbsp sunflower oil
½ tsp salt
1 Tbsp honey

Makes 7 Tbsp

61. Creamy herb

6 Tbsp sour cream
2 tsp fresh lemon juice
2 tsp fresh tarragon
1 tsp lemon zest

Can be used for beef and chicken.

Makes ½ cup

62. Lemon butter

3 Tbsp melted butter
1 Tbsp sunflower oil
1 tsp lemon zest
2 Tbsp fresh lemon juice
1 clove garlic, crushed
2 Tbsp chopped fresh parsley
1 Tbsp French mustard

Can be used for lamb, pork, chicken and seafood.

Makes ⅓ cup

63. For leg of lamb

3 Tbsp dry white wine
3 Tbsp fresh lemon juice
1 tsp lemon zest
3 Tbsp sunflower oil
1 clove garlic, crushed
a sprig each rosemary and origanum

Makes ½ cup

Bastes

GLAZES

Glazes are highly concentrated and are used to finish grilled or roasted cuts of meat. The glazes in this book are all sweet and are suited to smoked or fatty cuts of meat.

TIPS AND HINTS

- Glazes are usually used on smoked and fatty cuts of meat or poultry, as the acid in the sugar breaks down the fat and aids digestion.
- Glazes burn more quickly than marinades and bastes, and should only be used during the last few minutes of cooking.
- When glazing pork, remove the skin or crackling first before brushing the meat with a glaze.
- Unless stated otherwise, all the following glazes can be mixed by whisking, processing, shaking in a bottle (my favourite), blending or beating, provided they are smooth and free of any lumps.

BEEF

Steaks
Fillet (4 cm thick), Rump (2.5 cm thick), T-bone (2.5 cm thick), Sirloin (3 cm thick), Porterhouse (2.5 cm thick), Tornedos (2.5 cm thick), Chateaubriand (5–8 cm thick), Minute (1 cm thick)
SUGGESTED GLAZES: None, see marinades (page 10) and bastes (page 29)

Kebabs
SUGGESTED GLAZES: None, see marinades (page 10)

Whole cuts
Aitchbone, Flat rib, Fore rib, Prime rib, Rib-eye, Scotch fillet, Thick rib, Topside, Wing rib
SUGGESTED GLAZES: None, see marinades (page 10)

LAMB

Chops
Loin, Chump, Best end of neck, Saddle, Shoulder, Cutlets
SUGGESTED GLAZES: None, see marinades (page 10) and bastes (page 29)

Kebabs
SUGGESTED GLAZES: None, see marinades (page 10)

Whole spit-roast
SUGGESTED GLAZES: None, see bastes (page 29)

Whole cuts
Butterflied leg, Shoulder, Loin, Rolled loin, Ribs, Breast, Flank, Saddle, Rack
SUGGESTED GLAZES: None, see marinades (page 10)

PORK — FRESH, UNSMOKED

Chops
Loin, Neck, Cutlets, Escallops, Neck steaks, Leg steaks, Fillet, Ribs, Riblets
SUGGESTED GLAZES: Nos 64, 65, 66, 70, 71

Kebabs
SUGGESTED GLAZES: None, see marinades (page 10)

Whole cuts
Rib, Loin, Saddle, Neck (on the bone), Neck (deboned), eisbein, Hock/shank, Belly, Rolled belly
SUGGESTED GLAZES: None, see marinades (page 10)

Whole spit-roast
SUGGESTED GLAZES: None, see marinades (page 10) and bastes (page 29)

PORK — SMOKED, CURED

Chops and steaks
Kassler, Bacon, Neck, Gammon
SUGGESTED GLAZES: All

Whole cuts
Gammon, Spare rib, Loin, Neck
SUGGESTED GLAZES: Parboil first, then use any glaze

POULTRY

Baby chicken, Spring chicken, Turkey, Broiler
SUGGESTED GLAZES: Nos 64, 67, 70, 71, see marinades (page 11) and bastes (page 29)

Kebabs
SUGGESTED GLAZES: None, see marinades (page 11)

SEAFOOD

Line fish, Gamefish, Trawled fish
SUGGESTED GLAZES: None, see marinades (page 11)

Shellfish
SUGGESTED GLAZES: garlic or herb butter

Kebabs
SUGGESTED GLAZES: None, see marinades (page 11)

Glazes

64. Maple syrup

4 Tbsp maple syrup
½ cup brown sugar
1 tsp English mustard powder
white wine vinegar (enough to moisten)

Place all the ingredients in a bowl and whisk until smooth. This glaze can be used on pork or chicken.

Makes ⅔ cup

65. Apricot

2 tsp orange zest
4 Tbsp fresh orange juice
½ cup white wine vinegar
4 tsp brown sugar
1 tsp salt
12 canned apricot halves

Place all the ingredients, except the apricots, in a saucepan and bring to the boil. Boil until the mixture has reduced and starts to thicken. Place the apricots in a blender and blend until smooth, then stir into the boiled mixture. This glaze can be used on lamb or pork.

Makes 1 cup

66. Lemon

6 Tbsp sugar
6 Tbsp water
3 Tbsp fresh lemon juice
3 Tbsp apple juice
1½ Tbsp lemon zest
½ tsp salt

Place the sugar and water in a saucepan, bring to the boil and stir until the sugar dissolves. Add the remaining ingredients and whisk. This glaze can be used on pork, lamb or chicken.

Makes about 1¼ cups

67. Pineapple

1 x 440 g can crushed pineapple
⅔ cup soft brown sugar
1 Tbsp white wine vinegar
½ tsp salt

Place all the ingredients in a bowl and stir until well combined. This glaze can be used on pork or chicken.

Makes about 2 cups

Braai buddy

68. Coffee

⅓ cup strong black coffee
⅓ cup melted butter
2 tsp fresh lemon juice
1 tsp lemon zest

Place all the ingredients in a large bottle and shake vigorously. This glaze can be used on lamb.

Makes ⅔ cup

69. Raisin

3 Tbsp butter
1 Tbsp sunflower oil
1½ Tbsp brown sugar
2 tsp cornflour (Maizena)
2 Tbsp fresh lemon juice
¾ cup seedless raisins

Place all the ingredients in a food processor and process until smooth. This glaze can be used on any smoked cuts of meat, and is especially good on gammon steaks.

Makes about 1½ cups

70. Plum

1 x 410 g can stoned plums
½ tsp lemon zest
1 tsp brown sugar
½ tsp ground ginger
1 tsp fresh lemon juice

Place all the ingredients in a food processor and process until smooth. This glaze can be used on duck or pork.

Makes about 1½ cups

71. Apple cider

1 cup apple cider
2 Tbsp brown sugar
2 Tbsp honey
2 tsp mustard powder

Place all the ingredients in a large bottle and shake vigorously. This glaze can be used on pork, lamb, chicken, duck or venison.

Makes 1¼ cups

When glazing pork, remove the crackling first.

SAUCES

TIPS AND HINTS

- Sauces are usually used without marinades, bastes or glazes. If a sauce is to be served with meat that has been marinated, take care to choose a combination that does not clash.
- A sauce is not a gravy because it has a flavour of its own, unlike a gravy which gets its flavour from the residue of the meat with which it is to be served. A sauce is also usually thicker than a gravy.

Basic BBQ 1

1 large onion, chopped
2 cloves garlic, crushed
1 stick table celery, chopped
1 Tbsp sunflower oil
1 Tbsp butter
2 Tbsp red wine vinegar
1 Tbsp brown sugar
1 Tbsp tomato sauce
1 cup hot beef stock
1 Tbsp Worcestershire sauce
1 Tbsp mustard powder
½ tsp cayenne pepper
1 Tbsp fresh lemon juice

Sauté the onion, garlic and celery in the oil and butter until soft. Add the vinegar and sugar and simmer for 5 minutes. Add the remaining ingredients, except lemon juice, and simmer for 25 minutes until thick. Add the lemon juice

Makes 1½ cups

Basic BBQ 2

2 large onions, chopped
2 large cloves garlic, crushed
2 tsp chopped fresh root ginger
1 Tbsp sunflower oil
½ cup red wine vinegar
1 Tbsp brown sugar
1 cup hot beef stock
1 x 240 ml can tomato purée
1 Tbsp Worcestershire sauce
1 tsp salt
¼ tsp ground cloves
2 Tbsp fruit chutney
2 Tbsp dry sherry

Sauté the onions, garlic and ginger in the oil until soft. Add the vinegar and sugar and simmer for 5 minutes. Add the remaining ingredients and simmer for 25 minutes or until the sauce is thick.

Makes 4 cups

Traditional BBQ

1 onion, chopped
2 cloves garlic, finely chopped
2 Tbsp butter
2 sticks table celery, with leaves, chopped
4 Tbsp chopped green pepper
1 x 400 g can whole tomatoes
¾ cup tomato purée
2 Tbsp tomato paste
1 bay leaf
2 tsp mustard powder
1 tsp salt
½ tsp ground cloves
½ tsp ground allspice
⅓ cup brown vinegar
2 Tbsp fresh lemon juice
2 Tbsp dry sherry
2 Tbsp black treacle (molasses)
a few drops Tabasco sauce
1 Tbsp chopped fresh parsley
1 tsp dried mixed herbs

Sauté the onion and garlic in the butter until soft. Add the remaining ingredients and simmer for about 30 minutes. Cool and purée the mixture in a food processor or blender. This sauce can also be used as a baste for poultry, ribs, burgers, steaks and pork, and may be reheated and used as a sauce to accompany meat or poultry.

Makes 2½ cups

American BBQ

3 Tbsp Worcestershire sauce
1 tsp chilli powder
1 tsp mustard powder
1 tsp salt
1 tsp freshly ground black pepper
4 Tbsp honey
1 cup chilli sauce
1 cup tomato sauce
a couple of dashes Tabasco sauce
3 Tbsp red wine vinegar
6 Tbsp water
3 Tbsp tarragon vinegar

Place all the ingredients in a food processor and process until smooth. This sauce goes particularly well with steak, and can be heated if preferred.

Makes 3 cups

When using canned whole, peeled tomatoes in a sauce or potjie that requires slow simmering, do not break up the tomatoes until the simmering process is complete.

Worcestershire sauce

4 cups brown vinegar
5 Tbsp anchovy paste
½ tsp cayenne pepper
6 Tbsp fried, minced mushrooms
1 clove garlic, crushed
4 Tbsp soy sauce
3 onions, very finely chopped
a pinch of salt
1 tsp mustard powder

Place all the ingredients in a bottle and seal. Refrigerate. Shake 3 times a day for 2 weeks. Strain, bottle and store for up to 3 months.

Makes 4 cups

Spicy tomato relish

¾ cup tomato purée
3 Tbsp brown sugar
1 Tbsp prepared mild mustard
3 Tbsp white vinegar
½ tsp dried mixed herbs
1 Tbsp soy sauce
2 Tbsp HP sauce
a few drops Tabasco sauce

In a saucepan, bring all the ingredients to the boil and simmer for 10 minutes. Serve as an accompaniment to burgers, chops or steaks.

Makes 1⅓ cups

Remoulade

1 cup mayonnaise
2 Tbsp French mustard
1 Tbsp chopped gherkins
½ Tbsp chopped capers
½ tsp chopped fresh parsley
1 Tbsp chopped onion
1 tsp chopped fresh tarragon
½ tsp chopped anchovy or fish paste

Mix all the ingredients together and serve with fish dishes. This is much better than tartare sauce!

Makes about 1¾ cups

Sweet-and-sour 1

3 Tbsp soy sauce
2 Tbsp sugar
3 Tbsp red wine vinegar
2 Tbsp dry sherry
1¼ Tbsp cornflour (Maizena)
½ cup hot chicken stock

Place all the ingredients, except the cornflour and stock, into a saucepan and bring to the boil. Mix a little stock with the cornflour to make a thin paste. Add the remaining stock and the cornflour paste to the saucepan. Bring to the boil slowly and simmer until the sauce thickens, stirring constantly.

Makes 1⅓ cups

Braai buddy

Sweet-and-sour 2 (American)

1½ cups boiling water
3 Tbsp brown vinegar
1 Tbsp soy sauce
3 Tbsp chutney
3 Tbsp brown sugar
2 Tbsp tomato sauce
5 drops Tabasco sauce
2 tsp cornflour (Maizena)

Place all the ingredients, except the cornflour, into a saucepan and bring to the boil. Simmer until the sugar dissolves, stirring constantly. Mix enough water with the cornflour to make a paste. Remove the simmering mixture from the heat and gradually stir in the cornflour paste. Return the saucepan to the heat and stir continuously for about 1 minute or until the sauce thickens.

Makes 2 cups

- Steak is very rare or *bleu* when a firmly pressed finger leaves an indentation.
- Steak is rare to medium rare when it feels spongy and springy. Red meat continues cooking for a few minutes after being removed from the grill.
- Well-done steak will not be discussed in this book.

Sweet-and-sour 3 (Chinese)

⅓ cup soy sauce
1 cup brown sugar
¾ cup brown vinegar
½ cup dry sherry
2 Tbsp oyster sauce
1 green pepper, thinly sliced
1 Tbsp candied ginger, chopped
¾ cup pineapple pieces
2 Tbsp water
2 Tbsp cornflour (Maizena)

Place the soy sauce, sugar, vinegar, sherry, oyster sauce and green pepper into a saucepan and bring to the boil. Add the ginger and pineapple pieces. Mix the water and cornflour to form a paste. Remove the saucepan from the heat and stir in three-quarters of the cornflour paste. Stir well, then return to the heat, stirring all the time until thickened. If the sauce is too thin, add the remaining cornflour paste. Pour the sauce over the cooked meat and serve.

Makes 3½ cups

Sauces

Pesto

½ cup tightly packed fresh basil
¼ cup fresh origanum
4 Tbsp olive oil
4 Tbsp dry-roasted pine nuts
2 Tbsp grated Parmesan cheese
3 cloves garlic, peeled
a pinch of salt

Place all the ingredients in a blender and blend until almost smooth.

Makes ¾ cup

Note: To store for a few days, spoon into a jar and pour a little olive oil on top to prevent air reaching the pesto. Seal and refrigerate.

Garlic mayonnaise

2 egg yolks
2 cloves garlic, crushed
½ tsp French mustard
a pinch of freshly ground black pepper
1 cup sunflower or olive oil
4 tsp white wine vinegar

In a blender, blend together the egg yolks, garlic, mustard and pepper. While the machine is still running, gradually add the oil in a thin stream. Add the vinegar gradually (machine still running). Great with fish dishes.

Makes 1½ cups

Green pepper and tomato relish

½ cup olive oil
2 medium onions, sliced
4 cloves garlic, very finely chopped
6 green peppers, seeded and cut into thick strips
1 x 410 g can whole, peeled tomatoes, coarsely chopped
½ tsp salt
¼ tsp freshly ground black pepper

Heat the oil in a frying pan. Add the onions and fry until soft but not brown. Add the garlic and fry for 1 minute. Add the remaining ingredients and cook until the peppers are just tender. This sauce can be served hot or cold, and is also good as a topping for burgers and hot dogs.

Makes about 3 cups

Monkey gland

1 cup fruit chutney
2 Tbsp Old Brown sherry
2 Tbsp brown vinegar
½ tsp Peri-peri sauce (page 42)

Place all the ingredients in a saucepan, bring to the boil and serve with steaks and burgers.

Makes 1¼ cups

Braai buddy

Tomato

4 Tbsp sunflower oil
1 onion, finely chopped
½ stick table celery, finely chopped
½ carrot, finely chopped
2 cloves garlic, crushed
1.5 kg tomatoes, skinned*, seeded and chopped
1 bay leaf
1 tsp finely chopped fresh thyme
1 tsp finely chopped fresh origanum
1 tsp finely chopped fresh basil
1 Tbsp salt
1 tsp sugar
1 tsp white pepper

Heat the oil in a saucepan and fry the onion, celery and carrot until tender but not brown. Add the garlic and fry for 1 minute. Add the tomatoes, herbs and seasonings. Reduce the heat and simmer for 2 hours. Allow to cool, remove the bay leaf and process until smooth. The sauce can be frozen.

Makes about 4 cups

---

* Soak tomatoes in boiling water for 1-1¼ minutes. Drain, and when cool enough to handle, slice off the stem end and squeeze. The tomato should slip out of its skin and the seeds should shoot out the sliced-off end.

Italian tomatoes and red peppers

2 Tbsp olive oil
2 Tbsp butter
1 large onion, thinly sliced
2 cloves garlic, crushed
4 red peppers, seeded and cut into strips
4 large tomatoes, skinned and chopped
salt and freshly ground black pepper
1 tsp finely chopped fresh basil
1 tsp finely chopped fresh origanum
1 bay leaf

Heat the oil and butter in a saucepan and fry the onion until soft but not brown. Add the garlic and fry for 2 minutes. Add the red peppers and simmer, covered, for 15 minutes. Add the remaining ingredients and simmer, uncovered, for 20 minutes, or until the sauce begins to thicken. Remove the bay leaf and serve hot or cold.

Makes 1 cup

Never, ever, use a fork while braaiing, other than to stab a critic or meat poacher in the hand when they misbehave.

Sauces

Mushroom

500 g mushrooms (do not use button mushrooms if possible as these are the most bland)
200 g butter
½ cup sunflower oil
½–⅔ cup flour
4 cups warm milk
a pinch each salt, freshly ground black pepper and grated nutmeg
a sprig of fresh parsley
a sprig of fresh thyme
½ bay leaf
½ medium onion, peeled, stuck with a clove

Slice the mushrooms and fry them in the butter for 5 minutes, or until browned. Set aside. To make the roux (thickening agent), combine the oil and flour in a saucepan, stirring constantly until it reaches the consistency of thick porridge. Add the milk to the roux and bring to the boil, whisking constantly. Add the seasoning, herbs and onion, and reduce the heat. Simmer for 25–30 minutes over the lowest heat possible. Strain the sauce, then stir in the fried mushrooms, including the butter in which they were fried.

Makes 5 cups

Port

½ cup port
1 tsp fresh lemon juice
½ tsp soft green peppercorns, crushed
1 cup hot chicken stock
1½ Tbsp fresh cream
1 Tbsp butter

In a saucepan, bring to the boil the port, lemon juice and peppercorns and reduce to two-thirds of its original volume. Add the stock and cream and reheat, then stir in the butter. Serve with any steak or venison dish.

Makes 1¾ cups

Peri-peri

½ cup finely chopped fresh chillies
4 cloves garlic, crushed
2 tsp fresh lemon juice
2.5 cm-piece of lemon peel
1½ tsp coarse salt
1 Tbsp olive oil
1 Tbsp sunflower oil
1 Tbsp white vinegar

Bottle the ingredients and refrigerate for 12 days, shaking the container once a day. This sauce may be served warm (do not cook or boil it) or cold. To make a pourable sauce, add 1 heaped teaspoon to 1 cup of melted butter.

Makes about ¾ cup

should you overdose on peri-peri, avocado, banana or milk will help alleviate the burn.

Braai buddy

Apple

1/3 cup water
4 Tbsp sugar
2 tsp fresh lemon juice
1 x 410 g can pie apples

In a saucepan, bring the water, sugar and lemon juice to the boil. Stir until the sugar dissolves. Add the apples, bring to the boil, then reduce the heat and simmer for 5 minutes. Remove from the heat and cool. Mash or blend the apples until smooth.

Makes about 1 1/3 cups

Mint

1 cup tightly packed fresh mint leaves
4 Tbsp water
3 Tbsp white vinegar
2 Tbsp sugar
1/4 tsp salt

Chop the mint very finely. Set aside. Bring the remaining ingredients to the boil and stir until the sugar dissolves. Place the mint in a gravy boat and pour the hot liquid over the mint. Leave to stand for 2 hours or until cool.

Makes about 1 cup

Mustard

6 Tbsp sugar
4 eggs
2 Tbsp mustard powder
1 Tbsp flour
1 tsp salt
1 tsp white pepper
2/3 cup brown vinegar

Beat 5 Tbsp of the sugar and the eggs in a bowl. Combine the remaining sugar with the mustard, flour, salt and pepper. Place the sugar-egg mixture in a saucepan. Mix the vinegar into the dry mixture, then add this to the saucepan and heat slowly, stirring. When the sauce thickens, serve immediately.

Makes about 1 1/4 cups

Garlic butter

500 g butter, at room temperature
3 Tbsp fresh lemon juice
2 tsp salt
15–20 cloves garlic, crushed
2 Tbsp chopped fresh coriander leaves
2 dried red chillies, very finely chopped

Cream the butter, add the remaining ingredients and mix well. Spoon the mixture onto a square of greaseproof paper and roll into a sausage shape. Place in the fridge or freezer until firm. To use, simply slice off rings as required.
  To make herb butter, follow the same method but add chopped fresh origanum, thyme and parsley.

Makes 500 g

Sauces

Chillies

Paprika
The weakest chilli, about 12 cm long, green when young, changing to red. Usually ground to make powder. Heat rating out of 10: 1½

Pasilla
Originally from Mexico, green when young, changing to black. Heat rating out of 10: 2

French wax
Medium strength, about 10 cm long, green then red with a waxy appearance. Heat rating out of 10: 4

Bolivian rainbow
Medium strength, purple when growing then yellow to orange-red. Heat rating out of 10: 4

Pueblo
Used mainly in chilli powder. Heat rating out of 10: 5

De Arbol
Originally from Mexico, 7 cm long, thin shape, green then dark red. Heat rating out of 10: 7

Jalapeño
Originally from Mexico, dark green then bright red. Heat rating out of 10: 7½

Habanero yellow
Lantern-shaped in appearance, green then red or yellow. Heat rating out of 10: 10

Mexican chilli paste

16 assorted hot dried whole chillies, roasted, seeded and soaked*
1 medium onion, thinly sliced
2 cloves garlic, chopped
½ tsp cumin seeds, crushed (in a mortar and pestle)
1½ tsp coriander seeds, crushed
¼ tsp fennel seeds, crushed
½ tsp ground cinnamon
½ Tbsp coarse salt
1½ tsp roasted almonds
1½ tsp sesame seeds, dry-fried
1½ Tbsp seedless raisins
1 large tomato, skinned
½ slice stale white bread, cubed

Place the chillies, onion and garlic in a blender and blend until smooth. Gradually add the remaining ingredients while processing and blend until smooth. If the paste is too thick, add a little water.

Makes 2½ cups

---

* Roast in a preheated oven at 200 °C for 3–4 minutes. Make sure they do not burn. Remove the stems and seeds and cover with boiling water. Soak for about 20 minutes, then drain.

Braai buddy

Green Thai chilli paste

1 Tbsp coriander seeds
1 tsp cumin seeds
1 tsp black peppercorns
1 small onion, chopped
3 cloves garlic, chopped
2 stalks lemon grass, cut into thin strips and chopped
6 green chillies, topped and tailed
1½ Tbsp chopped fresh coriander leaves
1 Tbsp chopped fresh root ginger
zest of 2 limes
1 tsp anchovy paste
1 Tbsp brown sugar

Place the coriander seeds, cumin seeds and peppercorns in a frying pan and dry-fry for 2–3 minutes, shaking the pan continuously. Do not let them burn. Allow to cool, place in a mortar and pestle and grind into a powder. Place the powder and all the remaining ingredients in a processor and process until smooth.

Makes ¾ cup

Chilli oil

2 cups sunflower oil
10 whole fresh red chillies, stems removed

Heat the oil in a frying pan until hot enough to shrivel a sprig of parsley. Remove from the heat and add the whole chillies. Leave to stand overnight, then bottle and store in the fridge. The oil can be brushed over steaks, chops, and so on.

Makes 2 cups

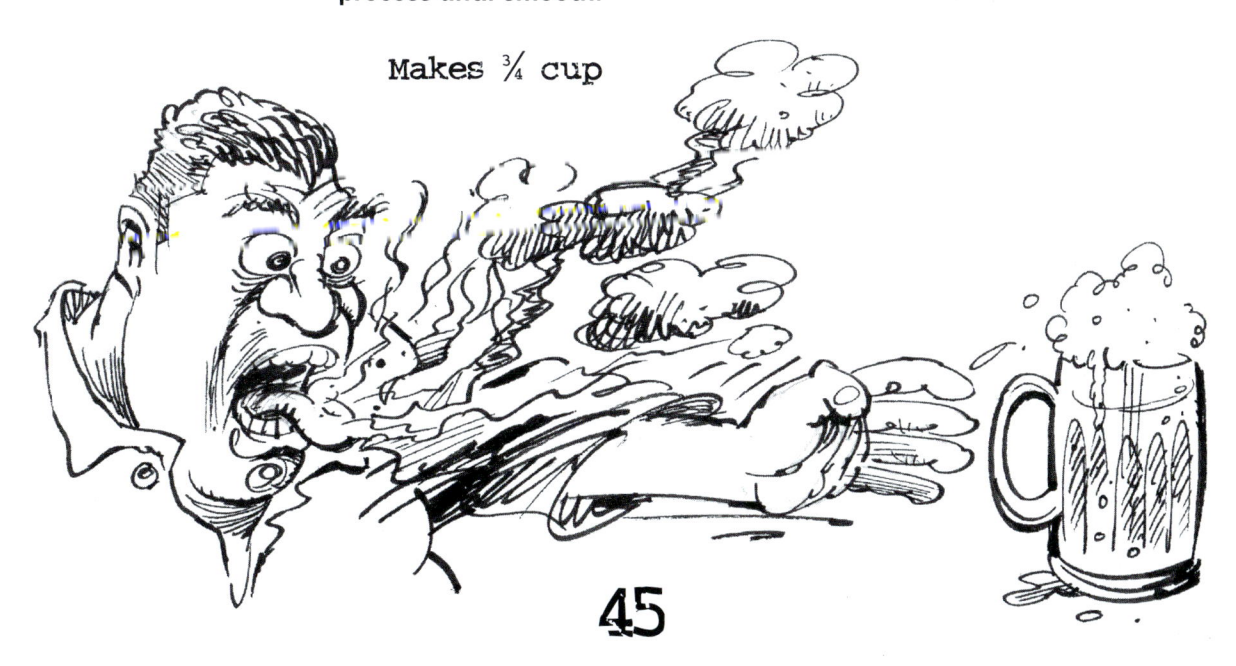

Do not criticise your host's cooking skills — he might actually know what he is doing — and remember: 'the proof of the pudding is in the eating'.

BURGERS

The humble burger or hamburger did not originate in the U.S.A. as most Americans would like us to believe, nor did it originate in Hamburg, Germany. It actually comes from Russia, where peasants were eating rissoles (meatballs) on bread long before America gained its independence.

TIPS AND HINTS

- Burgers are best grilled over hot coals or placed under a grill with a drip tray underneath.
- Should you wish to fry the burgers, a cast-iron, corrugated (griddle) pan is best.
- Avoid using too much oil when frying; the less the better.
- The flatter you make your burgers, the less oil will be required to fry them.
- If the burgers are to be frozen for later use, fry the onions in oil until soft and slightly brown. This will prevent the bitterness that comes from freezing raw onion. Do the same with the garlic.
- Always leave the mixture to stand for 1 hour before shaping into burgers, as this will allow the different flavours to combine.
- When shaping the patties, wet your hands often, as this prevents the burger mixture from sticking to your hands and also results in a smoother pattie.
- After shaping the burger patties with your hands, place them well apart on a large sheet of greaseproof paper. Cover with another sheet of greaseproof paper and roll out with a rolling pin so that each one is 2–2.5 cm thick.

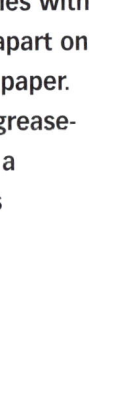

Braai buddy

Basic burger mix

1 kg beef topside, coarsely minced
2 medium onions, finely chopped
2 Tbsp finely chopped fresh parsley
1 Tbsp salt
½ tsp white pepper

Place all the ingredients into a large mixing bowl and combine thoroughly with your hands. Leave to stand for 1 hour, then shape into burgers. Fry, braai or grill for 4–8 minutes on each side, depending on how rare or how well-done you prefer your meat. Turn only once.

Makes 8 patties, or just over 1 kg

For medium to well-done burgers, grill until beads of blood appear on top, then turn and grill for another 3 minutes and serve.

Deluxe burger mix

2 medium onions, finely chopped and fried in oil until lightly browned
1 green pepper, seeded, finely chopped and fried in oil until soft
2 small green chillies, very finely chopped
1 fat clove garlic, crushed and chopped
4 Tbsp chopped fresh parsley
1 kg beef mince
1 cup fresh breadcrumbs
2 Tbsp tomato purée
1 Tbsp Worcestershire sauce
2 eggs, beaten
salt and freshly ground black pepper

Place all the ingredients into a large mixing bowl and combine thoroughly with your hands. Leave to stand for 1 hour, then shape into burgers. Fry, braai or grill for 4–8 minutes on each side, depending on how rare or how well-done you prefer your meat. Turn only once.

Makes 10 patties, or just over 1 kg

Burgers

OPTIONS AND VARIATIONS

Here are just 20 variations of the Basic burger mix on page 47 that can be created simply by adding or removing various ingredients or combinations of ingredients.

Mediterranean

To Basic burger mix add:

2 medium green peppers, seeded, finely chopped and fried in olive oil until soft

Chilli

To Basic burger mix add:

2 tsp chopped fresh green chillies, fried in oil until soft

Herb

To Basic burger mix add:

2 tsp finely chopped fresh thyme
4 tsp finely chopped fresh origanum or marjoram

Garlic

To Basic burger mix add:

4 cloves garlic, crushed and chopped

Spicy

To Basic burger mix add:

3 Tbsp Worcestershire sauce
4 Tbsp tomato sauce
1 Tbsp Tabasco sauce
1 Tbsp brown vinegar

Baste with Spicy tomato relish (page 38).

Cheese-stuffed

To Basic burger mix add:

1 cup loosely packed, grated strong Cheddar cheese

If frying, always use a non-stick pan.

Braai buddy

Onion

Omit the onions and salt from Basic burger mix and add:

4 Tbsp French onion soup powder

Mustard

Omit pepper from Basic burger mix and add:

2 tsp prepared mild mustard
4 Tbsp whole grain mustard
1 tsp freshly ground black pepper

Ranch

Omit the salt from Basic burger mix and add:

2 Tbsp beef stock powder

Lemon-tarragon

To Basic burger mix add:

4 Tbsp No. 4 Lemon and tarragon marinade (page 13)

Baste with the same marinade if grilling.

Boere or sausage

Use 750 g mince in Basic burger mix and add:

250 g sausage/boerewors meat (no casings)
1 tsp crushed coriander seeds

Country

To Basic burger mix add:

1 tsp crushed coriander seeds
1 tsp ground allspice

BBQ

To Basic burger mix add:

4 Tbsp American BBQ sauce (page 37)

Baste with the same sauce.

Pork

Use only 500 g beef mince in Basic burger mix and add:

500 g pork mince

When using tarragon, remember that it does not keep its flavour as well as most herbs when dried. If fresh tarragon is not available, choose another recipe.

Burgers

Lamb

Instead of using beef mince in Basic burger mix, use:

500 g pork mince
500 g lamb mince

Caribbean

To Basic burger mix add:

4 Tbsp No. 8 Caribbean marinade (page 14)

Baste with the same marinade.

Peri-peri

USE WITH CAUTION!
This recipe is for serious chilli munchers and not for those with a faint heart or palate.

To Basic burger mix add:

1 Tbsp Peri-peri sauce (page 42)

Teriyaki

To Basic burger mix add:

4 Tbsp No. 9 Teriyaki marinade (page 14)

Baste with the same marinade and serve with fresh pineapple slices.

Curry

To Basic burger mix add:

1 Tbsp meat masala

Baste with No. 3 Tandoori marinade (page 12).

Sosatie

Proceed as for lamb burger (above) but add 4 Tbsp No. 12 Sosatie marinade (page 15)

Baste with the same marinade.

Braai buddy

Accompaniments

The following may be served with or on the cooked burger:

Tomato slices	Grated strong cheese
Gherkin slices	Pineapple slices, grilled or raw
Radish slices	Coleslaw salad
Cucumber slices	Avocado slices
Onion rings, fried or raw	Salsas
Lettuce leaves	Banana slices, fried or raw

Condiments and sauces

The following may be served with or on the cooked burger:

Chutney	Traditional BBQ sauce (page 37)
Mayonnaise	American BBQ sauce (page 37)
Tomato sauce	Mustard
Chilli sauce	Sweet-and-sour sauce 2 (page 39)
Tabasco sauce	HP sauce
Basic BBQ sauce (page 36)	Burger relish

KEBABS

TIPS AND HINTS

- Always marinate cubes of meat, chicken or fish for at least 4 hours before threading onto skewers.
- When using wooden skewers, soak them in water for 2 hours before threading the meat.
- When using fish, make certain it is of the firm-fleshed variety, such as kingklip.
- When using prawns, they should be deveined and shelled before threading onto skewers.
- If available, cherry tomatoes are easier to work with than tomato wedges.
- When cooked, the meat cubes can be removed from the skewers and stuffed in pita envelopes.

Braai buddy

KEBAB INGREDIENTS

Meat: fat-free, boneless, cubed beef, lamb, chicken, pork, veal, fish, prawns, and so on, marinated for at least 4 hours before cooking; bacon cubes, rind removed, blanched in boiling water for 1 minute.

Vegetables: green, red or yellow peppers, cubed; button mushrooms; pearl, cocktail, pickling or baby onions; cherry tomatoes; whole tomatoes, quartered; green or black olives, stoned; courgettes (baby marrows), thickly sliced, sprinkled with salt and left to stand for 20 minutes, then rinsed thoroughly.

Fruits: pineapple pieces; dried apricots, soaked in water for 2 hours; dried apples, soaked in water for 2 hours; dried peaches, soaked in water for 2 hours; dried prunes, soaked in water for 2 hours, pips removed after soaking.

Kebab banquet

600 g pork fillet, cubed
600 g deboned leg of lamb, cubed
500 g chicken breast fillets, cubed
500 g smoked sausage, sliced
500 g thick, rindless streaky bacon rashers, cubed
250 g button mushrooms
500 g baby onions, peeled
2 green peppers, cubed
2 large pineapples, peeled, cored and cubed
250 g dried fruit, soaked in water for 2 hours

Marinade
½ cup soy sauce
½ cup honey
4 Tbsp tomato sauce
4 Tbsp brown vinegar
2 Tbsp dry sherry
2 Tbsp water
2 tsp brown sugar
2 tsp chicken stock powder
2 cloves garlic, crushed

Mix all the marinade ingredients together and marinate the pork, lamb and chicken in separate bowls. Place the remaining ingredients into individual bowls so that guests may create their own kebabs. Braai over medium to hot coals, turning and basting frequently with leftover marinade.

Serves 16–20

Shish kebabs 1

700 g lamb, deboned and cubed
1 red pepper, cubed
1 green pepper, cubed
20 cherry tomatoes
12 baby onions
1½ Tbsp sunflower oil

Marinate the meat in No. 13 Shish kebab marinade (page 15) for 4–6 hours. Drain the meat and reserve the marinade. Thread red pepper, meat, green pepper, tomatoes and onions alternately onto skewers. Brush with oil and cook slowly over medium coals, turning and basting occasionally with the marinade. Heat the remaining marinade and serve with the kebabs and rice.

Serves 4–6

Shish kebabs 2

1 kg deboned leg of lamb, trimmed of fat and cubed
1 large onion, sliced
1½ Tbsp double-thick cream
1 large tomato, quartered, or 4 cherry tomatoes
1 green pepper, quartered

Marinade
1½ tsp olive oil
3 Tbsp fresh lemon juice
5 tsp salt
½ tsp freshly ground black pepper

Combine the marinade ingredients and mix well. Add the lamb and onion and marinate for 2–4 hours, turning occasionally. Remove the lamb from the marinade (discard the onions and marinade) and tightly thread onto four skewers. Brush with cream. Thread the tomatoes and green peppers alternately onto separate skewers. Place the lamb skewers over hot coals and grill until done. Start grilling the tomato and pepper skewers about 5–7 minutes after starting the lamb, as they take less time to cook.

Serves 4

Pork 2

1 cup fresh orange juice
2 Tbsp chutney
1 Tbsp prepared mild mustard
2 tsp golden syrup
1 Tbsp chopped fresh rosemary
1 Tbsp chopped fresh origanum
4 pork neck steaks, 2.5 cm thick, trimmed of fat and cubed
1½ cups dried apricots, soaked in water for 2 hours
1½ cups canned pineapple pieces, drained
salt and freshly ground black pepper

Place the orange juice, chutney, mustard, syrup, rosemary and origanum in a bowl and whisk thoroughly. Place the pork, apricots and pineapple pieces in the mixture and stir to coat the meat and fruit. Marinate for 4–6 hours. Thread the pork onto skewers, alternating with the apricots and pineapple. Sprinkle salt and pepper over the skewers just before braaiing for 6 minutes per side over medium coals.

Serves 4

Moroccan

1.5 kg lamb, deboned and cubed
1 large onion, peeled and quartered
2 green peppers, quartered

Marinate the meat in No. 14 Moroccan marinade (page 15) for 4–6 hours. Thread the meat, onion and peppers onto skewers, leaving a little space between each ingredient. Braai over medium coals, turning and basting frequently. Serve with saffron rice or remove from the skewer and place inside a pita envelope.

Serves 10–12

Pork 1

1 kg pork steaks (fillet or neck), cubed
1 red pepper, cubed
1 green pepper, cubed
1 x 410 g can pineapple pieces

Marinate the meat in No. 33 Martini marinade (page 20) for 4 hours. Thread the meat, peppers and pineapple alternately onto skewers and braai over medium coals, turning and basting frequently.

Serves 6

> If you burn your fingers, fill a short whisky glass with ice and top up with cold water. Keep your fingers immersed for 20–30 minutes.

Kebabs

Lamb's kidney and liver

For each skewer
2 lamb's kidneys
3 squares lamb's liver

Skin, split and devein the kidneys. Skin, remove ducts and cut the liver into 2.5 cm cubes. Marinate the kidneys and liver in No. 15 Kidney and liver marinade (page 15) for 4–6 hours. Thread alternately onto skewers and braai for 6–8 minutes over medium to hot coals, turning and basting frequently. Both the kidneys and liver should be pink inside. Serve immediately.

1 kebab per person

Tropical beef

3 cloves garlic, crushed
2 tsp paprika
2 Tbsp olive oil
2 Tbsp fresh lemon juice
1 tsp ground ginger
1 tsp ground cinnamon
700 g rump steak, trimmed of fat and cubed
2–3 ripe mangoes, cubed
2 red peppers, cubed

Combine the garlic, paprika, oil, lemon juice, ginger and cinnamon, and whisk thoroughly. Pour the mixture over the cubed rump steak and marinate for 4–6 hours. Thread mango cubes, red pepper squares and steak alternately onto skewers. Braai for 8–10 minutes over hot coals, turning and basting occasionally.

Serves 4–6

Braai buddy

Lamb

1 kg deboned leg of lamb, cut into
2.5 cm cubes
4 rashers rindless bacon, cut into
2.5 cm cubes
2 green peppers, cut into 2.5 cm cubes
4 tomatoes, quartered
8 onions, quartered
16 bay leaves
16 button mushrooms

Marinate the lamb and bacon in No. 1 Greek-style marinade (page 12) or No. 12 Sosatie marinade (page 15) for 4–6 hours. Drain and pat dry using paper towels. Thread onto skewers in the following order: lamb, bacon, green pepper, tomato, onion, bay leaf and mushroom. Repeat until all the ingredients have been used. Braai over medium coals, turning and basting frequently.

Serves 4–6

Mixed meat

500 g deboned leg of lamb, cut into
2.5 cm cubes
500 g rump steak, cut into 2.5 cm cubes
8 lamb's kidneys, deveined and quartered
8 rashers rindless bacon, cut into
2.5 cm cubes
24 cocktail or pearl onions
8 tomatoes, quartered
3–4 green peppers, cut into 2.5 cm cubes

Marinate the lamb, rump, kidneys and bacon in No. 33 Martini marinade (page 20) for 4–6 hours. Drain and pat dry using paper towels. Thread onto skewers in the following order: lamb, onion, tomato, rump, kidney wrapped in bacon, green pepper. Repeat until all the ingredients have been used. Braai over medium coals, turning and basting occasionally.

Serves 4–6

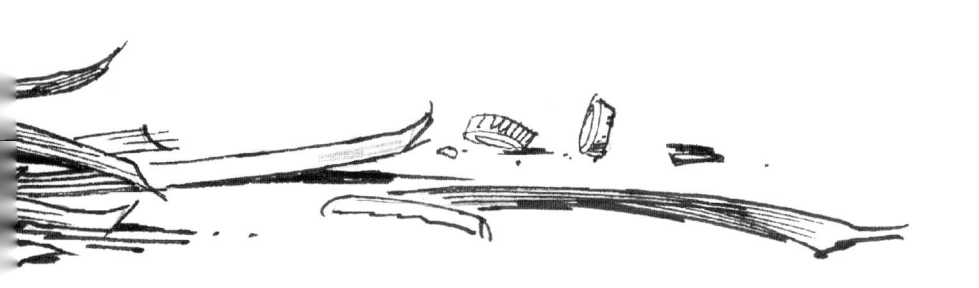

Kebabs

Venison

1 kg venison fillet, cut into 2.5 cm cubes
12 rashers rindless streaky bacon, cut into 2.5 cm cubes
2 large green peppers, cubed
2 large onions, quartered and soaked in water to separate the layers
1 x 410 g can pineapple pieces

Place the cubed venison in a bowl and marinate in No. 6 Red wine marinade (page 13) for 3 days. Thread venison, bacon, green pepper, onion and pineapple alternately onto skewers. Braai over medium to cool coals turning and basting occasionally.

Serves 4–6

Spanish

1 kg deboned shoulder of lamb, cut into 2.5 cm cubes
8 rashers rindless bacon, cut into 2.5 cm cubes
8 tomatoes, quartered or 32 cherry tomatoes
24 stuffed green olives
8 button mushrooms

Marinate the lamb and bacon in No. 34 Spanish kebab marinade (page 20) for 4–6 hours. Drain and pat dry using paper towels. Each person gets two skewers, skewer (a) and skewer (b). Thread lamb and bacon onto skewer (a), and tomatoes, olives and mushrooms onto skewer (b). Braai over medium coals, turning and basting frequently.

Makes 16 small kebabs

Parsley is an excellent natural breath freshener.

Braai buddy

Chicken

6 chicken breasts, deboned, skinned and cubed
1 green pepper, cubed
1 red pepper, cubed

Marinade
2 Tbsp soy sauce
2 tsp mustard powder
2 Tbsp soft brown sugar
2 Tbsp Madeira wine or medium-cream sherry
2 Tbsp olive oil

Combine all the marinade ingredients and blend in a processor. Place the chicken in a bowl, pour the marinade mixture over, and mix thoroughly. Marinate for 4–6 hours. Thread the chicken and peppers onto skewers and braai, basting frequently with the remaining marinade until done.

Serves 6–8

It is important to remember that, because chicken breasts contain almost no fat, this dish and others that contain chicken breasts, are particularly unforgiving for those who tend to overcook.

Chicken and pineapple

1 x 250 g pack rindless streaky bacon, halved crossways
1½ cups chicken livers, cleaned
6 chicken breasts, deboned, skinned and cubed
1 pineapple, peeled and cubed

Marinade
3 Tbsp sunflower oil
1 Tbsp white vinegar
1 Tbsp fresh lemon juice
4 Tbsp dry white wine
2 tsp soft brown sugar
3 Tbsp soy sauce
2 Tbsp tomato paste
1 Tbsp ground ginger
½ tsp freshly ground black pepper
¾ tsp salt

Wrap each bacon rasher half around a chicken liver. Combine all the marinade ingredients and mix well. Add the cubed chicken to the marinade and leave to stand for 2–4 hours. Thread the chicken cubes, bacon-wrapped livers and pineapple onto skewers. Braai for 10 minutes on each side, basting frequently.

Serves 6–8

Kebabs

SAUSAGES

DESCRIPTION OF VARIOUS SAUSAGES

Bratwurst: sausage made from pork, or pork and veal and seasoned with sage and lemon.

Thuringer: sausage made from pork and seasoned with sage, salt and pepper.

Bockwurst: sausage made from 70% veal and 30% pork, with milk and eggs and seasoned with parsley and chives.

Frankfurter: sausage made from finely minced beef and pork. The meat is salted, seasoned and sometimes smoked. Frankfurters are usually 2.5 cm thick.

Viennas: same as frankfurters, only 1.25 cm thick.

Bierwurst: sausage made from coarsely chopped pork, with or without garlic. It is about 4–5 cm thick and is usually served cold and thinly sliced with pickles and beer.

Russian: sausage made from coarsely chopped pork and seasoned with salt and paprika.

Grilled bratwurst

1–2 bratwurst per person

When grilling any thick German sausage that contains pork or veal, it is important to keep the skin intact. Place the sausages in cold water and heat gradually. Do not boil, otherwise the sausage will burst. Place the hot sausages on the braai and brown over a low heat for colour, turning only once (very gently).

The best boerewors ever (Peter Devereux)

1 kg boerewors
½ cup brown vinegar
1 cup muscadel or jerepigo

Place the boerewors in a plastic container, then pierce the sausage all over with a fork. Mix the vinegar and sweet wine, and pour it over the boerewors. Leave to marinate for 24 hours in the fridge. Braai as you would regular boerewors.

Serves 4

Boerewors (farmer's sausage)

3 Tbsp whole coriander seeds
1.5 kg deboned beef
1.5 kg deboned pork
5 tsp salt
1 tsp freshly ground black pepper
½ tsp ground cloves
½ tsp grated nutmeg
500 g spek (the layer of fat between the skin and the flesh; loin of pork is best)
⅔ cup brown vinegar
90 g sausage casings

Scorch*, grind and sift the coriander. Cut the meat into 5 cm cubes and mix with the remaining ingredients, except the spek, vinegar and casings. Mince the meat and dice the spek into 3 mm cubes. Add the spek and vinegar to the minced meat and mix lightly but thoroughly. Fill the casings loosely.

Serves 24

---

* Either dry-roast on a tray in the oven at a high temperature, or dry-fry in a hot pan until the coriander starts turning brown and gives off a strong aroma.

Boerewors is done when the fat inside boils to the top of the sausage during cooking.

Sausages

Karoo wors (country sausage)

3 kg deboned beef
2 Tbsp salt
4 Tbsp whole coriander seeds, scorched, ground and sifted
1 Tbsp ground cloves
½ tsp grated nutmeg
1½ tsp freshly ground black pepper
1 tsp dried thyme
1.5 kg spek (pork fat)
7 tsp dry white wine
1 Tbsp fresh lemon juice
110 g sausage casings

Cut the meat into strips and pack in layers in a large bowl. Place all the spices and herbs in a mortar and pestle and grind thoroughly. Sprinkle over the meat and leave to stand overnight. Mince the meat and half the pork fat. Cut the remaining pork fat into 3 mm cubes and add to the meat together with the wine and lemon juice. Fill the casings loosely.

Serves 30

Pork sausage

3 kg shoulder of pork, deboned
2 kg belly of pork, deboned and rind removed
1 tsp white pepper
½ tsp ground allspice
½ tsp grated nutmeg
1 tsp onion flakes
1 tsp coriander seeds, crushed
1 Tbsp salt
4 Tbsp fresh lemon juice
4 Tbsp each dry white wine and white vinegar, mixed
120 g pork sausage casings

Cut the meat into small cubes, add the dry seasonings and lemon juice and mix well. Put the meat through a coarse mincer or pulse lightly with a processor. Add the wine-vinegar mixture, mix well and stuff loosely into sausage casings.

Serves 20

Never prick a sausage, unless otherwise specified, before or during cooking as the juice and fat contains most of the flavour.

Braai buddy

Bockwurst

1.5 kg lean pork
2.5 kg lean veal
2 Tbsp fresh lemon juice
1 tsp dried sage
6–8 Tbsp chopped fresh parsley
3 Tbsp white pepper
2 Tbsp fine salt
a large pinch of grated nutmeg
a large pinch of ground cloves
1 Tbsp white sugar
1 egg
⅓ cup milk
100 g sausage casings

Dice the meat into 2 cm cubes and toss with the lemon juice, herbs, spices and sugar, then mince once. Beat the egg with the milk and mix lightly into the meat. Fry a teaspoon of the mixture to test for seasoning. If satisfactory, fill the casings and tie into 15 cm lengths. Cook the sausages in very hot, simmering water for 10 minutes, then cool in cold running water. Dry with paper towels and store in the fridge.

Serves 12

Always ensure that your partner eats the same amount of garlic as you do!

Sausages

POTJIEKOS

Although typically South African, potjiekos is thought to have originated in Europe during the 80 Year War (1568–1648), when a shortage of food during the siege of Leiden forced the inhabitants to cook almost anything that they could lay their hands on in one communal pot. The South African pioneers adopted this method of cooking, not due to a shortage of food, but because it was convenient and it suited their lifestyle of travelling and hunting. Traditionally, a three-legged cast-iron pot was used. Remember that making potjiekos is a social event. Cooking time could be anything from 2–6 hours, thus requiring much patience and tolerance (back-seat drivers beware!), so set aside an afternoon or evening for this type of entertainment. I have taken the liberty of adding a few dishes that are not traditional potjiekos recipes.

POTJIEKOS INGREDIENTS

Beef: neck, shin, brisket, flat rib, short rib, flank, bolo, chuck, blade, topside, silverside and oxtail.

Lamb and mutton: neck, shank, flank and breast.

Pork: shank, trotters, head, belly and thick rib.

Venison: any cut will do.

Fish and chicken: any firm-fleshed fish, such as kingklip, can be used. Any portion of or whole chicken can be used.

Aromatic vegetables: onions, carrots and celery, usually fried in oil or fat, with spices and herbs added later.

Bulk vegetables: potatoes, sweet potatoes, turnips, dried fruit, rice.

Stock or liquid: beef or chicken; or 1 stock cube to 2 cups boiling water, or add wine.

Fuel or wood: The type of fuel or wood used is not important as the pot is covered and the food is not affected by the wood's aroma. Any type of wood, charcoal, coal, briquettes, etc. can be used if it burns for a long time. Once you have browned the meat and onions, a potjie requires only minimal heat to complete cooking.

You might prefer to have a second or back-up fire on hand, so that coals can be added or removed in order to regulate the heat under the potjie.

COOKING INSTRUCTIONS

one: Place the pot over the coals and heat.

two: Add enough oil, fat, dripping, lard or bacon fat to moisten the bottom of the pot.

three: When the oil is very hot, add the meat and fry on all sides until brown.

four: Add the onions, celery, carrots and garlic, and fry until just turning brown.

five: Add the herbs and spices, and fry for a further 2 minutes.

six: Add the wine or stock to just below the level of the meat and simmer. If you add too little stock, you can always add more later. The meat will shrink by 25% during cooking and too much liquid will dilute the gravy.

seven: Adjust the heat by removing coals. You only need 4–5 coals to keep it at a simmer.

eight: Add bulk vegetables in layers in order of cooking time. Add the vegetables with the longest cooking time first.

nine: Cover the pot with a lid, open your second beer and relax.

ten: Do not stir, poke or fiddle with the potjie while cooking. Leave it alone! You may occasionally lift the lid to see if it is still simmering and not boiling. Do not let it simmer dry. If necessary, add a little liquid to maintain the moisture content.

A potjie is similar to a stew or bredie, so remember: 'A stew boiled is a stew spoiled'.

Garlic tends to go slightly bitter when fried or sautéed for more than a minute, so ensure that most of your frying is done before adding garlic.

Oxtail

3 Tbsp sunflower oil
1 oxtail, jointed
2 large onions, chopped
2 sticks table celery, sliced diagonally
1 bay leaf
2 tsp chopped fresh thyme
1 Tbsp chopped fresh parsley
salt and freshly ground black pepper
1 tsp paprika
¾ cup red wine
1⅔ cups beef stock (or use 1 beef stock cube to 500 ml boiling water)
3 Tbsp tomato paste

Heat the oil in a pot, add the oxtail and brown all over. Remove coals to reduce the heat. Add the onions and celery, and fry until soft. Add the herbs and spices and fry for a further 2 minutes. Add the red wine and cook for 5 minutes. Add the remainder of the ingredients. Cover and simmer for 3–4 hours, or until the meat almost falls off the bone.

Serves 4–6

Mutton

1 Tbsp sunflower oil
500 g breast of mutton, cut into portions
500 g blade of beef, cubed
2 medium onions, chopped
2 cloves garlic, crushed
½ tsp chopped fresh rosemary
½ tsp chopped fresh thyme
1 bay leaf
1 tsp salt
½ tsp freshly ground black pepper
1½–2 cups hot beef stock
1 x 410 g can whole tomatoes, chopped
1 small bunch spinach, washed, stems removed and coarsely chopped
500 g potatoes, peeled and quartered
5 pickling onions, peeled

Heat the oil in a pot, add the meat and brown all over. Add the onions and garlic and fry until soft. Add the herbs and spices, and fry for 2 minutes. Add the stock and tomatoes, cover and simmer for 2 hours. Add the remaining vegetables and simmer until the potatoes are tender.

Serves 4–6

Braai buddy

Pork and lentil

3 Tbsp sunflower oil
1 kg breast of pork, cut into portions
2 large onions, chopped
2 cloves garlic, crushed
1 stick table celery, chopped
2 tsp salt
½ tsp freshly ground black pepper
1 tsp chopped fresh rosemary
1 bay leaf
2 medium tomatoes, peeled and chopped
3 cups hot beef stock
3 carrots, sliced
250 g smoked sausages
400 g brown lentils, soaked

Heat the oil in a pot, add the pork and brown all over. Add the onions, garlic and celery and fry until soft. Add the remaining ingredients, except the sausages and lentils, cover and simmer for 1½–2 hours, or until the meat is nearly tender. Pierce the sausages all over to prevent bursting, and add to the pot together with the lentils. Simmer for a further 40 minutes, or until the lentils are tender.

Serves 6

Lamb and tomato

6 Tbsp sunflower oil or dripping
1.5 kg lamb on the bone (neck, rib or shin)
4 rashers rindless bacon, sliced into strips
4 medium onions, chopped
2 medium carrots, chopped
3 cloves garlic, crushed
1 Tbsp chopped fresh basil
1 Tbsp chopped fresh origanum
1 tsp paprika
1 tsp ground coriander
½ tsp caraway seeds
1 tsp salt
½ tsp freshly ground black pepper
½ tsp sugar
1 x 410 g can whole tomatoes, chopped
1½ cups hot beef stock
8 medium potatoes, peeled, quartered and parboiled

Heat the oil or dripping in a pot, add the meat and brown all over. Add the bacon and fry for 2 minutes. Add the onions, carrots and garlic, and fry until slightly browned. Add the herbs, spices and sugar, and fry for a further 2 minutes. Add the remaining ingredients, except the potatoes, and simmer for 2–3 hours, or until the meat is almost tender. Add the potatoes and simmer for 10 minutes.

Serves 6–8

Jambalaya

2 Tbsp olive oil
300 g rindless bacon, diced
2 cups uncooked rice
1 onion, chopped
2 medium green peppers, cut into strips
16 cloves garlic
4 tomatoes, skinned and chopped
1 tsp dried thyme
1 tsp salt
1 tsp freshly ground black pepper
2 1/3 cups hot chicken stock
500 g prawns, shrimps, mussel meat or chicken
fresh coriander leaves to garnish

Heat the oil in a pot and fry the bacon slowly until crispy. Remove and set aside. Add the rice and sauté for 6–8 minutes. Add the onion and sauté for another 3 minutes. Add the green peppers and cook slowly, stirring frequently until softened. Add the garlic, tomatoes, thyme, fried bacon and seasoning. Add the chicken stock, then cover and simmer for 10–15 minutes. Add the seafood or chicken and cook, covered, until the rice has absorbed all the liquid. Garnish with coriander and serve.

Serves 8–10

Chilli con carne

4 Tbsp olive oil
2 large onions, finely chopped
2 sticks table celery, coarsely chopped
1 medium green pepper, coarsely chopped
4 medium chillies, seeded and finely chopped
3 cloves garlic, crushed
1 kg beef mince
½ tsp ground cumin
1 x 70 g can tomato paste
½ cup dry white wine
a pinch of salt
1 x 410 g can baked beans in tomato sauce

Heat the oil in a pot, add the onions, celery, green pepper, chillies and garlic. Fry gently until soft but not brown, then spoon the mixture to the side of the pot to make space for the mince. Add the mince and fry in one piece without stirring until the underside is brown. Once this is achieved, break up and stir the mince, and continue frying for a few minutes. Add the remaining ingredients, except the baked beans, cover and simmer for 1½–2 hours. Pour the baked beans into a strainer and rinse under a cold tap to remove *all* the sauce. Add the washed baked beans to the pot 5 minutes before serving.

Serves 4–6

Steak and stout

4 Tbsp olive oil
1.25 kg braising steak, cubed
2 onions, chopped
2 cloves garlic, crushed
2 medium carrots, sliced
4½ Tbsp flour
1⅕ cups Guinness or milk stout beer
4 Tbsp tomato purée
1⅕ cups hot beef stock
1 Tbsp chopped fresh thyme
zest of 1 orange
½ tsp ground allspice
½ tsp ground cloves
250 g brown mushrooms, sliced and fried in butter
salt and freshly ground black pepper

Heat the oil in a pot and fry the meat until brown all over. Remove the meat from the pot and set aside. Add the onions, garlic and carrots to the pot and fry until soft. Stir in the flour and fry slightly. Add the Guinness or stout, tomato purée and beef stock, stirring continuously. Return the beef to the pot with the thyme, orange zest, allspice and cloves. Cover and simmer for 2 hours, or until the meat is tender. Add the mushrooms 10 minutes before the end of the cooking period and check seasoning.

Serves 6–8

Waterblommetjie

2 Tbsp sunflower oil
1.5 kg lamb on the bone
4 medium onions, chopped
1 clove garlic, crushed
2 whole cloves
1 small stick cinnamon
2 tsp salt
a large pinch of freshly ground black pepper
1 bay leaf
1 Tbsp flour
1¼ cups hot beef stock
500 g waterblommetjies, washed, rinsed thoroughly and stems removed
6 medium potatoes, peeled, quartered and parboiled

Heat the oil in a pot and fry the meat until brown all over. Add the onions and garlic, and fry until soft. Add the spices and bay leaf and fry for 2 minutes. Sprinkle flour over the meat and onion mixture, and fry, stirring a few times to make sure that the flour is also fried slightly. Reduce the heat and add the beef stock. Cover and simmer for about 1½ hours, then add the waterblommetjies and potatoes, and simmer for a further 30 minutes, or until the waterblommetjies are tender. Once the waterblommetjies and potatoes have been added, stir as little as possible to avoid breaking up the potatoes.

Serves 6–8

Never braai unless you are wearing shoes or sandals. Hot coals and bare feet don't mix.

Chicken liver

6 Tbsp olive oil
6 medium onions, coarsely chopped
2 cloves garlic, crushed
1 kg chicken livers, cleaned
2 tsp Tabasco sauce
1 tsp coarse salt or ½ tsp fine salt
6 Tbsp dry white wine

Heat the oil in a pot and fry the onions and garlic until soft but not brown. Remove the onions and garlic and set aside. Increase the heat, add the livers to the pot and fry until brown (be careful because they tend to spit when frying). Add the remaining ingredients, including the onion mixture, cover and simmer for 10 minutes. This dish can be served on toast or rolls, or with pasta or rice.

Serves 6–8

Chicken and garlic

40 cloves garlic, unpeeled
½ cup olive oil
2 tsp chopped fresh parsley
2 tsp chopped fresh origanum or marjoram
1 tsp chopped fresh thyme
½ tsp coarse salt
freshly ground black pepper
1 x 2 kg whole chicken
3 Tbsp fresh lemon juice
6 Tbsp dry white wine
6 Tbsp water

Place the garlic, oil, herbs and spices into an *unheated* pot. Place the whole chicken on top of this, then turn over a few times so that the chicken is completely coated with the oil, herbs and spices. **Place the chicken breast-side up.** Pour the remaining ingredients *around the sides* of the chicken. Cover with a tight-fitting lid and simmer at the lowest heat possible for 3–4 hours. *It is very important to have a lid that fits tightly or flush with the pot to prevent any aroma or flavour from escaping.* If this is difficult due to an ill-fitting lid, then cover the top half of the pot and lid with aluminium foil to improve the seal. After 3–4 hours of simmering, the chicken should have collapsed and almost disintegrated, now completely overcooked. Do not panic, as this is the intention!

The meal may be served in two ways. It may be dished into individual bowls with plenty of the juices, and served with Portuguese rolls or ciabatta. Alternatively, the pot may be used to dip the rolls or bread into, at the same time snaring the odd piece of chicken while doing so. Do not be alarmed at the quantity of garlic as it is neither peeled nor crushed.

Serves 4–6

Braai buddy

Chicken à la king

650 g chicken breasts, deboned, skin removed and cut into thick strips
2 Tbsp fresh lemon juice
2 Tbsp butter
2 Tbsp sunflower oil
2 onions, chopped
1 green pepper, seeded and chopped
1 clove garlic, crushed
½ cup dry white wine
⅔ cup hot chicken stock
1 Tbsp French mustard
a sprig of fresh thyme
250 g brown mushrooms, sliced
⅔ cup fresh cream
3 Tbsp cornflour mixed with 3 Tbsp water to form a paste
salt and freshly ground black pepper

Place the chicken in a bowl, pour the lemon juice over, coat thoroughly and set aside for 30 minutes. Remove the chicken and allow to drip dry. Heat the butter and oil in a pot and fry the chicken until brown all over. Remove the chicken, add the onions and green pepper, and fry until soft. Return the chicken to the pot with the garlic, and stir-fry for 1 minute. Stir in the wine and cook for another minute, then stir in the stock, mustard and thyme. Cover and simmer for 10 minutes. Add the mushrooms and simmer for 10 minutes. Stir in the cream and bring back to a simmer. Remove from the heat and gradually stir in the cornflour paste. Return to the heat and bring back to a simmer, stirring continuously, until the sauce has thickened. Check seasoning and serve.

Serves 4–6

Chicken and ginger

2 Tbsp sunflower oil
8 chicken thighs
2 large onions, coarsely chopped
2 large green peppers, cut into 8 strips each
2 small chillies, finely chopped
4 cloves garlic, crushed
4 cups ginger ale
a pinch of salt

Heat the oil in a pot. Add the chicken and fry until brown all over. Add the onions, green pepper, chillies and garlic and fry until just brown. Add the ginger ale and cook uncovered over a medium to high heat, until the liquid has reduced to a thick, sticky syrup, about 1 hour. Once the liquid has reduced by about two-thirds there is a chance that the chicken will burn due to the sugar in the ginger ale. Stir gently but frequently, turning the chicken over occasionally. The end result should be a glazed chicken dish that is well browned. Check seasoning and serve.

Serves 4

When using parsley as a breath freshener, always brush your teeth afterwards as the green leaves, when chewed, tend to colour your teeth.

De Waal's chicken

2 Tbsp olive oil
4 rashers streaky bacon, rind removed, sliced into strips
1 large onion, chopped
3 large leeks, white part only, sliced
1 stick table celery, plus leaves, chopped
1 large green pepper, chopped
1 large red pepper, chopped
1 large carrot, chopped
1–2 large green chillies, very finely chopped
3 cloves garlic, crushed
2 Tbsp finely chopped fresh origanum
1 Tbsp finely chopped fresh basil
salt and freshly ground black pepper
1 x 1.5 kg whole chicken, with giblets
1 chicken stock cube dissolved in 6 cups boiling water
1 x 410 g can whole tomatoes, chopped
1–1½ cups uncooked rice
½ cup frozen peas

Heat the oil in a pot. Add the bacon and fry until crispy. Add the onion, leeks, celery, peppers, carrot, chillies and garlic, and fry until soft but not brown. Add the herbs, salt and pepper and fry for 1 minute. Rinse the inside of the chicken with hot water and place it, breast-side up, on top of the vegetable mixture. Add the stock and tomatoes, cover and simmer for 45 minutes. Add the rice and simmer for 30 minutes. Add the peas and simmer until tender, about 5 minutes. Cut the chicken into sections in the pot (it should be tender enough to pull apart with two spoons), and stir gently to combine all the different colours and flavours. Serve in large soup bowls with Portuguese rolls or ciabatta bread.

Serves 6–8

Clanwilliam

4 Tbsp sunflower oil
1.5 kg breast of lamb, cut into portions
3 onions, chopped
1 Tbsp curry powder
a pinch each of ground cloves and grated nutmeg
2 tsp salt
1 x 283 g can pineapple rings, juice reserved
½ cup black rooibos tea
⅔ cup beef stock

Heat the oil in a pot, add the meat and brown all over. Add the onions and fry until soft. Add the curry powder and seasoning, and fry for 2 minutes. Add the remaining ingredients, cover and simmer for about 2 hours.

Serves 6–8

Braai buddy

Portuguese beef

2 kg wing rib or prime rib
1 kg baby potatoes
3 spicy sausages, sliced
3 carrots, sliced
10–15 black olives
grated nutmeg

Marinade
3 onions, chopped
1½ Tbsp sunflower oil
2 cloves garlic, crushed
4 ripe tomatoes, chopped
1 bay leaf
2 tsp paprika
salt and white pepper
1 tsp ground cumin
3 whole allspice
2 whole cloves
1 stick cinnamon
a sprig of fresh thyme
2 cups red wine

Place the meat and all the ingredients for the marinade in a cast-iron pot. Mix well and leave for 3–4 hours. Add the vegetables and olives and sprinkle with nutmeg. Cover and cook very slowly for 2–3 hours, or until the meat is tender.

Serves 6–8

Eastern beef

4 Tbsp olive oil
650 g topside or aitchbone, cubed
2 medium onions, coarsely chopped
2 sticks table celery, chopped
1½ cups hot beef stock
2 Tbsp soy sauce
1 green pepper, seeded and chopped
2 cups sliced brown mushrooms
1 Tbsp cornflour mixed with 1 Tbsp water to form a paste
1 cup pineapple pieces

Heat the oil in a pot and brown the meat on all sides. Remove the meat and set aside. Add the onions and celery to the pot and fry until soft. Return the meat to the pot, add 1 cup of stock and the soy sauce and simmer, covered, for 1–1½ hours, or until the meat is tender. Add the green pepper and the mushrooms and simmer for another 10 minutes. Remove the pot from the heat and add the cornflour mixture, stirring to combine. Add the pineapple pieces, heat through and serve.

Serves 6

Potjiekos

Mediterranean lamb

When using fresh basil and rosemary, remember that the flavour of these herbs increases in strength during cooking, so use sparingly.

4 Tbsp olive oil
3 lamb necks
4 Tbsp brandy
2 large onions, sliced
2 leeks, thinly sliced
3 sticks table celery, chopped
2 Tbsp chopped garlic
2 carrots, thinly sliced
4 sprigs fresh rosemary
4 bay leaves
18 baby potatoes, peeled
1 red pepper, cut into strips
1 green pepper, cut unto strips
250 g brown mushrooms, quartered
250 g courgettes (baby marrows), thickly sliced
12 pickling onions
12 sun-dried tomatoes
250 g black olives
3 Tbsp grated Parmesan cheese
½ cup chopped fresh parsley

Sauce

2 x 410 g cans chopped tomatoes
3 cups red wine
2 cups hot beef stock
2 Tbsp Aromat
2 Tbsp dried mixed herbs
1 Tbsp lemon pepper
1 Tbsp sugar

Heat the oil in a pot and brown the meat on all sides. Add the brandy and stir. Arrange the onions, leeks, celery and garlic on top of the meat. Add the carrots, rosemary, bay leaves and potatoes. Combine all the ingredients for the sauce, and whisk or blend in a processor. Pour the sauce over the meat and vegetables. Cover and simmer slowly for 1½–2 hours. Add the peppers, mushrooms, courgettes, pickling onions, sun-dried tomatoes and olives, and simmer for another 30 minutes. Add the Parmesan cheese and the parsley, stir gently and serve.

Serves 6

Mutton and cabbage

1 cabbage, shredded
4 Tbsp sunflower oil
1 kg deboned, cubed mutton, all fat removed
4 onions, chopped
2 tsp cumin seeds
4 whole cloves
2 whole allspice
salt and freshly ground black pepper
1½ cups hot beef stock
1 tsp sugar
8 baby potatoes, peeled
2 leeks, sliced
1 stick table celery, sliced
1 green chilli, seeded and very finely chopped

Place the cabbage in boiling, salted water and boil for 5 minutes. Drain, rinse under cold water and set aside. Heat the oil in a pot and brown the meat on all sides. Remove the meat and set aside. Add the onions and the spices to the pot and fry until the onion is soft. Return the meat to the pot, add the stock and the sugar, and simmer, covered, for 1½–2 hours or until the meat is just tender. Add the potatoes, leeks, celery, chilli and cabbage, and simmer for another 30 minutes, or until the potatoes are tender. If desired, serve chutney on the side.

Serves 6

Pork and pineapple

3 Tbsp sunflower oil
1 kg lean pork, cubed
2 medium onions, finely chopped
1 green pepper, seeded and coarsely chopped
2 Tbsp very finely chopped fresh root ginger
2 whole cloves
2 sticks cinnamon
1 bay leaf
2 cloves garlic, crushed
2 Tbsp red leaf masala or curry powder
2 cups uncooked rice
1 Tbsp apple cider vinegar
4 cups hot chicken stock
2 x 440 g cans pineapple pieces
3 Tbsp fresh lemon juice
salt and freshly ground black pepper

Heat the oil in a pot and brown the meat on all sides. Remove the meat and set aside. Add the onions, green pepper, ginger and whole spices to the pot and fry until slightly browned. Return the meat to the pot, add the garlic and masala or curry powder and stir-fry for another minute. Add the rice and mix well to combine. Add the vinegar, stock, pineapple pieces and lemon juice. Cover and simmer slowly for 50–60 minutes or until the rice has absorbed most of the liquid. Check seasoning and serve. This can be served with the same accompaniments as curry.

Serves 6–8

Mussel

4 Tbsp olive oil
1 onion, finely chopped
3 cloves garlic, finely chopped
2 tsp chopped fresh origanum
¼ tsp freshly ground black pepper
½ tsp salt
¼ tsp sugar
4 Tbsp chopped fresh parsley
1 cup dry white wine
2 x 410 g cans chopped tomatoes
2 cups hot chicken stock
750 g mussel meat

Heat the oil in a pot. Add the onion and fry slowly until soft but not brown. Add the garlic and origanum, and fry for 1 minute. Add the pepper, salt, sugar and parsley and fry for another minute. Add the wine, tomatoes and stock and bring to the boil. Cover and simmer for 10–15 minutes. Add the mussel meat, bring to the boil, and simmer for 5 minutes. Serve with Portuguese rolls or crusty bread.

Serves 4–6

Pumpkin

4 Tbsp sunflower oil
1.2 kg stewing lamb, cubed
salt and freshly ground black pepper
2 onions, sliced
3 cloves garlic, crushed
2 cm-piece fresh root ginger, grated
1 tsp ground cumin
1 tsp chopped fresh coriander
2 sticks cinnamon
1 Tbsp chopped fresh thyme
1 small green chilli, chopped
1 kg pumpkin, peeled and cubed
1 tsp brown sugar
½ cup hot water (only if necessary)

Heat the oil in a pot. Season the meat with salt and pepper and brown all over. Add the onions, garlic and ginger and fry slowly until the onions are brown. Add the cumin, coriander and cinnamon and stir-fry gently. Add the remaining ingredients, except the water, cover, reduce the heat and simmer slowly until the meat is tender. Check occasionally to see if water is needed. Serve with rice.

Serves 6–8

Braai buddy

Green bean curry

1 Tbsp sunflower oil
500 g stewing steak, cubed
2 onions, finely chopped
2 cloves garlic, crushed
1 tsp chopped fresh root ginger
4 tsp curry powder
1 tsp turmeric
1 Tbsp brown sugar
1 tsp fresh lemon juice
salt and freshly ground black pepper
1 cup hot beef stock
1 x 410 g can French-style green beans, drained or 250 g fresh green beans

Heat the oil in a pot and brown the meat all over. Remove the meat and set aside. Add the onions, garlic and ginger to the pot and fry until slightly brown. Return the meat to the saucepan and add curry powder, turmeric, sugar, lemon juice, salt and pepper. Stir-fry for about 5 minutes. Add the stock, reduce the heat, cover and simmer for about 1½ hours or until the meat is nearly tender. If using fresh green beans, add them now and simmer for another 30 minutes. If using canned beans, add them when the meat is tender, heat through and serve.

Serves 6–8

Lamb curry

4 Tbsp sunflower oil
1 kg stewing lamb, cubed
4 medium onions, chopped
2 green chillies, seeded and very finely chopped
2 tsp finely chopped fresh root ginger
2 tsp finely chopped garlic
1 tsp sugar
2 Tbsp curry powder
½ cup chopped dried apricots
½ cup sultanas
2 Tbsp brown vinegar
2 tomatoes, chopped
2 cups hot beef stock
a pinch of salt

Heat the oil in a pot. Add the meat and fry until brown all over. Remove the meat and set aside. Add the onions and chillies to the pot and fry until almost brown. Add the ginger, garlic, sugar and curry powder, and fry for 2 minutes. Add the apricots, sultanas and vinegar, and fry for 2 minutes. Add the tomatoes and stock, cover and simmer for 1½–2 hours or until the meat is tender. Check seasoning and serve.

Serves 6–8

FISH AND SEAFOOD

I have included a small fish section, mainly because no self-respecting Capetonian could compile a braai book without including a few fish recipes. I have also included a few Portuguese recipes, for the simple reason that, when it comes to cooking fish, I believe that they are the best.

Some local sea- and freshwater fish that are suitable for braaiing: angelfish, bass, bream, Cape salmon, carp, elf, galjoen, grunter, harder, kabeljou, maasbanker, mackerel, pilchards, sardines, seventy four, silverfish, snoek, steenbras, stumpnose, trout, tuna, yellowtail.

Crustaceans and shellfish: clams, crab, crayfish, langoustines, mussels, oysters, prawns.

Marinated calamari (Italian-style)

500 g calamari tubes or rings

Marinade
6 Tbsp olive oil
6 Tbsp fresh lemon juice
salt and freshly ground black pepper
1 Tbsp chopped fresh origanum
2 Tbsp soy sauce

Combine all the marinade ingredients and marinate the calamari for 3–4 hours in the fridge. Remove the calamari from the marinade, drip dry and braai for 3–5 minutes, turning only once during the cooking process. The calamari can also be cooked on a very hot, flat, cast-iron plate for about 1 minute.

Serves 3–4

Kaapse snoek

1 x 410 g can apricot jam
1 m² brown paper, or a square large enough to wrap up whole snoek
1 large fresh whole snoek, flecked

Use your fingers to cover the inside of the brown paper with a 5 mm-thick layer of apricot jam. Roll the whole snoek diagonally in the apricot jam-smeared brown paper to form a parcel. Sprinkle the outside of the parcel with plenty of water or vinegar. Place the snoek parcel on top of cool coals and cook for 8–10 minutes on each side, or place the parcel on top of a braai grid over medium coals, and cook for 8–10 minutes on each side. Turn only once.

Allow 150–200 g per person

When grilling fish, leave the skin on so if it sticks to the grill, only the skin will be left behind.

Grilled sardines (sardinanhas assadas)

24 whole, fresh sardines
1 cup coarse salt (no substitutes!)

Wash the sardines, but do not gut or scale them. Sprinkle with coarse salt and place in layers in a large bowl for 1 hour. Tilt the bowl so that the liquid runs off and shake off any excess salt before braaiing. Place the sardines in a hinged grill and secure. Braai the sardines on both sides over medium to hot coals until brown, about 2–3 minutes per side.

Serves 4

Fish and seafood

Grilled skewered swordfish (Turkish-style)

750 g swordfish, filleted, skinned and cut into 2.5 cm cubes
20 large bay leaves, soaked in boiling water for 1 hour

Marinade
½ tsp freshly ground black pepper
1 onion, cut into thick slices
3 Tbsp fresh lemon juice
1 Tbsp olive oil
1½ tsp salt

Combine the ingredients for the marinade and mix well. Add the fish and marinate for 2–4 hours in the fridge, turning occasionally. Remove the fish from the marinade, and drain the bay leaves. Tightly thread the cubes of fish and bay leaves alternately onto four skewers. Brush with the marinade and grill for 8–10 minutes until done.

Serves 4

Grilled angelfish (Portuguese-style)

1 kg angelfish, filleted, skinned and cut into 4 portions

Marinade
6 Tbsp butter
2 Tbsp dry white wine
2 Tbsp fresh lemon juice
salt and freshly ground black pepper
2 tsp chopped fresh parsley
2 tsp chopped fresh origanum
2 cloves garlic, crushed

Melt the butter in a saucepan and add the wine and lemon juice. Add the remaining marinade ingredients, stir well and remove from the heat. Do not cook or boil. Marinate the fish for 1–2 hours in the fridge, turning often. Grill over medium heat until done.

Serves 4

Fish is done when the juice that flows from it is milky, or the flesh flakes.

Braai buddy

Greek pickled fish

1.2 kg hake, filleted and cut into 16 portions
2 Tbsp fresh lemon juice
4 Tbsp sunflower oil
1 clove garlic, crushed

Sauce
2 onions, chopped
1 cup olive oil
5 cloves garlic, chopped
1 x 410 g can chopped tomatoes
3 Tbsp sultanas
salt and freshly ground black pepper
1 tsp dried mixed herbs
1 tsp sugar
4 Tbsp white vinegar
4 Tbsp dry white wine
⅔ cup sunflower oil
10–12 stoned black olives

Place the fish in an ovenproof dish, in a single layer. Combine the lemon juice, oil and garlic, and pour over the fish. Refrigerate for 1 hour. Place the uncovered dish with marinade in a preheated oven and bake at 180 °C for 35 minutes, or until done.
For the sauce, fry the onions in the olive oil until translucent. Add garlic and fry for 1 minute. Add the tomatoes, sultanas, salt, pepper, herbs and sugar and simmer for 3–4 minutes. Add the vinegar, wine and sunflower oil, and simmer for 5 more minutes. Add the olives. Place the fish in a non-metal container, cover with sauce and refrigerate for 24 hours.

Serves 6

Cape pickled fish

⅓ cup sunflower oil
1.2 kg yellowtail, filleted and cut into 8 portions
3–4 onions, sliced
2 green chillies, seeded and very finely chopped
1 Tbsp curry powder
½ tsp turmeric
4 Tbsp sultanas
1 Tbsp brown sugar
1 cup brown vinegar
5 Tbsp water
1 Tbsp smooth apricot jam or mild chutney
2 bay leaves
salt and white pepper

Pour half the oil into a frying pan and heat. Fry the fish in the oil until done. Remove the fish from the pan and drain on paper towels. Using a clean frying pan, fry the onions in the remaining oil until soft and brown. Add the chillies, curry powder, turmeric, sultanas and sugar, and fry for 1 minute, stirring continuously. Add the vinegar, water, jam or chutney, bay leaves, salt and pepper, and stir well. Simmer the sauce, uncovered, for 10 minutes. Pour a little sauce into a large glass dish and place the fish on top of the sauce, in a single layer, then pour the remainder of the sauce over the fish. Cover and refrigerate for 2 days before serving. This dish will keep for another 3–4 days if kept at 4–6 °C.

Serves 4–6

If you cut yourself or have an open wound, ensure that raw fish does not come into contact with the wound as this will cause a severe infection.

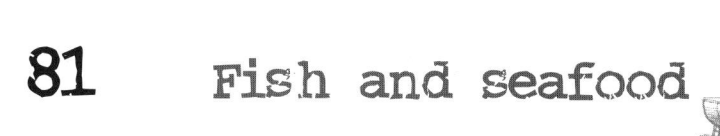

Fish and seafood

FAVOURITE RECIPES

Portuguese chicken livers

4 Tbsp olive oil
2 onions, finely chopped
2 cloves garlic, crushed and chopped
1 kg chicken livers, cleaned
½ tsp ground cumin
¼ tsp ground cloves
1 tsp paprika
1 bay leaf
1–2 whole dried red chillies, finely chopped
1 tsp coarse or ½ tsp fine salt
6 Tbsp dry white wine

Heat the oil in a pan and fry the onions until soft but not brown (about 4 minutes). Add the garlic and fry for 1 minute. Remove the onions and garlic from the pan and set aside. Add the chicken livers to the pan and fry until brown. Return the onion and garlic to the pan with the remaining ingredients and simmer for 6 minutes. Serve with Portuguese rolls or bread.

Serves 4–6

Portuguese beef skewers (espatadas)

1 kg rump steak, cut into 5 cm cubes
3–4 cloves garlic, crushed
2 tsp coarse salt
2 bay leaves
2 tsp freshly ground black pepper
bay leaf sticks or skewers
herb or garlic butter, melted

Place the meat in a bowl and season with garlic, salt, bay leaves and pepper. Leave for 30 minutes. Thread the cubes of meat onto bay leaf sticks or skewers. Brush with herb or garlic butter and grill for 5–6 minutes on each side. For the purist, it is essential to use bay leaf branches sharpened into skewers, then soaked in water for 1 hour, before threading.

Serves 4–6

Braai buddy

Lourenzo Marques chicken peri-peri

4 Tbsp butter
3 whole dried red chillies
2 tsp fresh lemon juice
2 cloves garlic
½ tsp paprika
2 tsp olive oil
1 tsp coarse salt
1 x 1.5 kg chicken, spatchcocked
(split down the back and spread flat)

Sauce
2 cloves garlic
1 Tbsp butter
1 Tbsp olive oil
1 dried red chilli, finely chopped
1 Tbsp fresh lemon juice
1 tsp chopped fresh parsley

Combine the butter, chillies, lemon juice, garlic, paprika, oil and salt, and blend in a processor. Spread over both sides of the chicken and leave to stand for at least 2 hours in the fridge. Grill over medium coals, turning occasionally until done.
For the sauce, fry the whole garlic cloves slowly in the butter and olive oil for about 2 minutes. Stir in the remaining ingredients, then remove and discard the garlic. Serve hot with the chicken.

Serves 4

Mozambique chicken peri-peri

3 cloves garlic, crushed
1 tsp coarse salt
1 tsp paprika
1 bay leaf
3 dried red chillies, finely chopped
2 cups coconut milk (add 3 cups desiccated coconut to 3 cups milk, simmer for 2 minutes, then strain)
1 x 1.5 kg chicken, halved and thicker parts slashed with a knife
2 Tbsp fresh lemon juice
4 Tbsp butter
4 Tbsp olive oil

Place the garlic, salt, paprika, bay leaf and chillies into a bowl and mix to form a paste. Add the coconut milk and mix. Place the chicken in the mixture and marinate for 10–12 hours in the fridge. Remove the chicken from the marinade and set aside. Add the lemon juice, butter and olive oil to the marinade, and bring to the boil. Remove from the heat and set aside to be used as a baste. Grill the chicken over medium coals, turning and basting often.

Serves 4

Use salt and oil to crisp chicken skin, pork crackling or jacket potatoes, as the salt dehydrates the skin during cooking.

Favourite recipes

Thai chicken

4 chicken breasts, skinned
2 cloves garlic, crushed
a handful chopped fresh parsley
1 Tbsp chopped fresh mint
2 tsp ground cumin
2 tsp ground coriander
1 chilli, seeded and chopped
juice and zest of 1 lemon
2 tsp soft brown sugar
1 cup coconut milk
2 tsp coarse salt

Make 3–4 incisions in each chicken breast and place in a shallow dish. Process all the remaining ingredients in a blender, and pour over the chicken. Ensure that the chicken is completely coated with the marinade, then leave for 1 hour in the fridge. Braai for 3–4 minutes, then turn the chicken over and braai for a further 3–4 minutes or until done.

Serves 2–4

Spare ribs

2 kg smoked pork rib
4 cups No. 58 Spare rib baste (page 30)

Place the smoked rib in a large pot, cover with water and slowly bring to the boil. Remove any scum that surfaces. Cover and simmer for 20 minutes. Drain off the water and add enough *heated* spare rib baste to cover the meat. Leave to cool together, as this will help impregnate the meat with the baste. The meat is already cooked so just braai over medium coals until browned to your liking. When finished, strain the remainder of the basting sauce, bring to the boil and simmer for 10 minutes. Allow to cool, then store in the fridge for up to 6 months (shake the bottle once a week).

Serves 4 (the quantities might seem large but bear in mind that spare rib is 80% bone)

Grilled leg of venison

1 x 1–1.5 kg deboned leg of venison

Marinade
1 cup sunflower oil
1 cup fresh lemon juice
2 Tbsp Aromat
1 tsp chopped fresh rosemary
1 clove garlic, chopped
freshly ground black pepper

Mix all the marinade ingredients together and pour over the meat. Marinate for 2–3 days in the fridge. Grill over medium coals for 1–1½ hours until completely cooked. This dish should be served well-done.

Serves 3–4

Grilled eisbein

Place the eisbein in a deep saucepan and cover with cold water. Bring to the boil slowly, removing any scum, and simmer until tender (1½–2½ hours). Pierce with a skewer to check if tender. Allow to cool in the liquid. When cool enough to handle, remove the skin with a sharp knife, leaving a thin layer of fat. Brush with any of the glazes (pages 33–35) and cook on the grill over a medium heat until well browned.

1 per person

Mediterranean rack of lamb

2 Tbsp mustard powder
1½ tsp coarse salt
2 tsp freshly ground black pepper
2 racks of lamb, each with 8 chops, trimmed of excess fat
4 Tbsp olive oil

Sauce
¾ cup olive oil
4 Tbsp fresh lemon juice
2 tsp dried origanum
2 cloves garlic, crushed
2 Tbsp chopped fresh parsley
salt and freshly ground black pepper

Sprinkle the mustard powder, salt and pepper over the meat and rub in well. Brush with olive oil. Blend all the ingredients for the sauce in a processor. Grill the racks of lamb, fatty side up, for 15–20 minutes or until medium done. Slice the racks into chops and pour the sauce over. Leave for 5 minutes and serve.

Serves 6–8

Do not apply salt to meat until the cooking is nearly completed, as this dehydrates the meat.

Glazed lamb breast

1 Tbsp brown sugar
¾ cup coarse salt
½ tsp saltpetre
1.5 kg whole breast of lamb

Combine the sugar, salt and saltpetre and rub into the meat. Place in a bowl in the fridge for 2 days. Remove the meat and hang in a draught or close to a fan, to dry on the outside. Place the meat in a saucepan, cover with cold water and bring to the boil. Simmer for 1½ hours or until the meat is tender. Remove from the water and cool. Dry thoroughly with paper towels. Braai slowly over medium coals for 20 minutes on each side. Brush with any of the glazes on pages 34–35, and braai for another 5 minutes on each side or until the meat is brown. Take care not to burn the glaze.

Serves 4–6

Lamb steaks

4 large lamb leg chops, 5 cm thick, round bone removed
4 Tbsp olive oil
2 Tbsp white wine vinegar
1 Tbsp coarsely chopped fresh mint
½ cup dry white wine
2 cloves garlic, crushed and chopped
freshly ground black pepper

Flatten the lamb chops with a steak mallet until about 2.5 cm thick. Combine the remaining ingredients in a bowl and whisk. Add the lamb chops, turning to coat all over. Leave to stand for 5 hours in the fridge. Cook over a medium to high heat.

Serves 4

Grilled beef marrow bones

Brush both sides of the marrow bones with sunflower oil or No. 62 Lemon butter baste (page 31). Place on grill over medium heat for a few minutes. When the marrow starts shrinking to form a meniscus, add a few drops of lemon juice and a grind of black pepper (only if using sunflower oil). When the marrow starts bubbling, cook for another 3–5 minutes, then remove *gently* with a spatula. *Do not turn the marrow bones as the marrow could fall out.* Serve immediately.

Braai buddy

Lamb souvlaki

500 g leg of lamb, deboned, fat removed and cubed
4–6 pita breads, pocket cut open

Marinade
1 medium onion, finely chopped
3–4 cloves garlic, crushed and finely chopped
4 Tbsp olive oil
1 tsp ground cumin
¼ tsp dried thyme
1 tsp dried origanum
½ tsp Peri-peri sauce (page 42)
1 tsp freshly ground black pepper

Sauce
¾ cup Bulgarian yoghurt
2 tsp fresh lime or lemon juice
½ tsp paprika

Garnish
1 small crisp lettuce, finely shredded
1 small onion, finely chopped

Place all the marinade ingredients in a bowl and mix well. Add the cubed lamb and marinate for 24 hours in the fridge. Thread the marinated lamb onto skewers and grill for about 6 minutes, turning occasionally. Mix all the sauce ingredients together. Place a little of the garnish inside the pita pocket, add some meat and sauce and serve.

Serves 4

Middle Eastern leg of lamb

1 leg of lamb, butterflied

Marinade
1 Tbsp finely grated fresh root ginger
2 Tbsp finely chopped fresh coriander
1 Tbsp curry powder
2 tsp ground cumin
2 Tbsp chutney
4 cloves garlic, crushed
1 Tbsp tomato paste
1 Tbsp melted butter
1¼ cups plain yoghurt
1 chilli, finely chopped

Blend all the marinade ingredients in a processor until well combined. Place the meat in the marinade and refrigerate for 24 hours. Braai over medium coals for 40 minutes per side. Don't turn too often, as the marinade should be allowed to form a crust on top.

Allow 200 g per person

Favourite recipes

SKOTTEL COOKING

Mediterranean sausage fry

4 Tbsp olive oil
4 large cloves garlic, unpeeled
8 sausages, about 15 cm long
4 onions, peeled and quartered
3 red, green or yellow peppers, quartered (or use all three for colour)
4 large tomatoes, quartered
3 large brown mushrooms (keep whole)
3 Tbsp chopped fresh origanum
a dash of dry white wine
salt and freshly ground black pepper

Place the oil and whole garlic into a cold skottel. Heat, stirring the garlic to flavour the oil. When the garlic starts sizzling, remove and discard. Add the sausages and brown. Add the onions and peppers, and fry until just going brown. Add the tomatoes, mushrooms and origanum, and reduce the heat. Cook for 5 minutes, stirring occasionally. Sprinkle with wine and cook for another 5 minutes or until the sausages are done. Check seasoning and serve.

Serves 4–6

Chinese pork stir-fry

2 Tbsp sunflower oil
500 g deboned pork, trimmed of fat and cut into strips
1 onion, thinly sliced
1 stick table celery, sliced diagonally
1 Tbsp brown sugar
1 Tbsp soy sauce
1 Tbsp brown vinegar
1 Tbsp dry sherry
⅓ cup bean sprouts
1 tsp salt
¼ tsp freshly ground black pepper

Heat the oil in a skottel until it smokes. Add the meat strips and brown all over. Add the onion and celery and stir-fry for about 5 minutes. Add the sugar, soy sauce, vinegar and sherry, and fry for 30 seconds. Add the bean sprouts and stir-fry for 2 minutes. Season and serve immediately.

Serves 4–6

Braai buddy

Chicken stir-fry

4 Tbsp sunflower oil
4 chicken breasts, deboned, skinned and sliced into thin strips
1 large onion, sliced
1½ cups topped, tailed and sliced French-style green beans
1 green pepper, chopped
2–3 carrots, sliced
2½ cups sliced brown mushrooms
3 courgettes (baby marrows), sliced
2½ cups bean sprouts
a few frozen peas
6 spring onions, including green part, chopped
2 cloves garlic, crushed
2–3 red chillies, chopped
2 Tbsp soy sauce
salt and freshly ground black pepper
2 tsp ginger juice (juice extracted from grated fresh root ginger)
1 cup cashew nuts, coarsely chopped

Heat the oil in a skottel until it smokes. Add the chicken and fry for a few seconds, stirring continuously. Add all the vegetables, garlic and chillies, and cook for 3–4 minutes, stirring continuously. Add the soy sauce, salt, pepper and ginger juice, and stir for a few more minutes. Sprinkle nuts over each serving and serve immediately.

Serves 4–6

Chicken and orange stir-fry

2 Tbsp soy sauce
2 Tbsp dry sherry
8 spring onions, cut into 5 cm-long pieces
1 tsp finely chopped fresh root ginger
¼ tsp ground ginger
¼ tsp white pepper
6 chicken breasts, deboned, skinned and cubed
¾ cup fresh orange juice
½ tsp brown sugar
a large pinch of salt
1 Tbsp cornflour (Maizena)
4 Tbsp sunflower oil
1 carrot, scraped clean and sliced lengthways in thin strips (julienned)

Combine the soy sauce, sherry, spring onion, both gingers and pepper, and mix well. Add the chicken pieces, stir to coat all over and leave to stand for 1 hour in the fridge. Combine the orange juice, sugar, salt and cornflour, mix well and refrigerate for 1 hour. Heat the oil in a skottel and stir-fry the carrot strips for 2–3 minutes or until just going brown. Remove the carrots and drain on paper towels. Add the chicken and stir-fry for 3–4 minutes. Add the orange juice mixture and stir-fry for about 5 minutes or until the sauce thickens slightly. Mix in the carrots strips and serve immediately.

Serves 4

Skinned chicken is healthier and enables the marinade to penetrate deeper, making for much tastier flesh.

Skottel cooking

Vegetable stir-fry

4 Tbsp sunflower oil
2 Tbsp mustard powder
1½ Tbsp grated fresh root ginger
4 cloves garlic, crushed
1 green chilli, finely chopped
2 tsp turmeric
1 tsp ground cumin
1 onion, thickly sliced
½ cup topped, tailed and sliced French-style green beans
½ cup thinly sliced green pepper
½ cup 2 cm-pieces table celery
¾ cup broccoli florets
¾ cup cauliflower florets
¾ cup thinly sliced brown mushrooms
2 Tbsp soy sauce
½ cup dry sherry

Heat the oil in a skottel and fry the mustard powder, ginger, garlic, chilli and spices for 30 seconds. Add the remaining ingredients, except the soy sauce and sherry, and stir-fry for 3–5 minutes or until tender. Add the soy sauce and the sherry and stir-fry for 1 more minute. Serve immediately.

Serves 4–6

Skottel-fried chicken pieces

4 Tbsp sunflower oil
8 chicken thighs
2 large onions, sliced into thick rings
2 large green peppers, sliced into thick rings
4 cloves garlic, crushed
2 chillies, finely chopped
4 cups ginger ale
a pinch of salt

Heat the oil. Add the chicken and brown. Add the onions, peppers, garlic and chillies, and fry until just brown. Add the ginger ale and cook, uncovered, for 1 hour until the liquid has reduced to a thick syrup, turning the chicken occasionally.

Serves 4–6

Skottel-fried chops

4 Tbsp sunflower oil
8–12 thick lamb chops, fat slashed
sprinkling of coarse salt
sprinkling of mustard powder
sprinkling of Worcestershire sauce

Heat the oil. Coat the chops in the salt, mustard powder and Worcestershire sauce, then fry over medium to high heat until done. Serve immediately.

Serves 4–6

chicken is done when the juice that flows from it is clear.

Braai buddy

The drinking man's skottel-fried breakfast

This dish is not recommended for those who have a cholesterol problem,
but is rather for those who are planning a 'heavy' day, alcohol-wise.

½ cup sunflower oil
8 rashers rindless streaky bacon
4 pork sausages
4 thin beef sausages, 15 cm long
2 onions, coarsely chopped
2 large tomatoes, halved
250 g whole brown mushrooms
4 lamb's kidneys, halved and cleaned
8 eggs
8 slices toast, buttered
2 x 500 mg capsules Vitamin C per person
1 x large capsule Vitamin B complex per person
4 cups strong coffee (optional)
4 tots rum or brandy (optional)
8 tsp brown sugar (optional)

Heat the oil. Fry the bacon until done, then set aside and keep warm. Reduce the heat to low and add the pork sausages. Cook for 5 minutes, turning frequently. Add the beef sausages and onions. Cook for 5 minutes. Remove all the sausages and onions, and keep warm. Place the tomatoes around the edge of the skottel, with the mushrooms in the centre. Cook for 5 minutes, turning the mushrooms frequently and the tomatoes only once. Remove and keep warm. Cook the kidneys for 2–3 minutes on each side. Coordinate your breakfast so that all the other ingredients are ready by the time the kidneys are done. (Kidneys should eaten immediately or they will toughen.) If you decide to serve an early breakfast, the optional ingredients may be taken at a later stage during the day.

Serves 4

Beef and ginger stir-fry

1 tsp ground ginger
1½ Tbsp soy sauce
1 tsp cornflour (Maizena)
½ tsp brown sugar
500 g rump or sirloin steak, cut into thin strips
2 tsp sunflower oil
5 cm-piece fresh root ginger, finely chopped
½ cup sliced brown mushrooms

Combine the ground ginger, soy sauce, cornflour and sugar, and mix well. Pour the mixture over the meat and leave to stand for 2 hours in the fridge. Remove the meat and allow to drain. Heat the oil in a skottel until it smokes. Add the meat and the root ginger and brown all over. Add the mushrooms and stir-fry for 5 minutes. Serve immediately.

Serves 4–6

Skottel cooking

SPIT-ROASTING

TIPS AND HINTS

- Always keep a second fire going to be used as a feeder fire.
- Place most of the coals at the front and rear of the spit because the legs and shoulders take the longest to cook as they are the thickest parts.
- The meat should be at least 60 cm above the fire.
- Always start with a few coals and add more later if necessary. You can always speed up the cooking process if too slow, but remember you cannot slow it down if it is too hot.
- Spit-roasting for the first timer is very much a 'trial and error' process, so be patient.
- Pierce the thickest part of the hind leg with a skewer to check the progress. When the juice runs clear, the meat is cooked.
- Remove from the spit and allow to rest for 10 minutes before carving.
- The hotter the fire, the faster the spit should rotate.

PORK TIPS

- Cooking time for pork is about 50 minutes per kilogram, but this can vary due to many factors, including the prevailing wind, the type of wood used, the heat of the fire, the type of container used for the coals, the height of the pig above the fire, etc. It also depends on whether the meat is stuffed (I don't recommend this for novices) or the chest cavity is opened or splayed Argentinean-style.
- Traditionally, the Portuguese do not score the skin when spit-roasting, although I would recommend scoring when using a baste.
- If the skin cooks too quickly and is almost crackling, remove it by peeling it off (set aside and keep it warm). However, you must then baste the meat regularly with a mixture of 20% oil to 80% dry white wine or apple juice.

LAMB TIPS

- Lamb is far thinner and the carcass less dense than that of pork, so the cooking time is less, about 20 minutes per kilogram.
- Baste every 10–15 minutes.
- If you wish to slow down the cooking process, particularly over the rib or loin section, cut aluminium foil to the shape of the area in question and secure with toothpicks, *shiny surface up*. The same applies to areas that might have been burnt from too fierce a fire in the early stages.

IF OVEN-ROASTING INSTEAD OF SPIT-ROASTING:

- If the piglet bends or twists in the oven, which is often the case, soak a dishcloth in ice-cold water, fold double and cover the area opposite the bend. Leave the dishcloth on the piglet until it dries out, about 5 minutes. This will cause the skin to contract and should straighten the bend. This process might have to be repeated a few times.
- If the pig is stuffed it will not bend, but you must then add 25% onto the cooking time.
- Measure the width of your oven before buying the piglet – this is a crucial factor! If you cannot find a piglet small enough, ask the butcher to remove the head as this makes up about a quarter of the length.
- Oven roasting time is 40–50 minutes per kilogram, unstuffed.
- Oven roasting time for a stuffed piglet is 60–70 minutes per kilogram.
- When using stuffing, always stuff loosely as the stuffing will expand by 20%.
- Allow to rest for 10 minutes before carving.

Place fresh herbs on the coals while grilling. The flavour will permeate the meat.

Spit-roasting

Pork

1 x 12 kg pig

Baste

4 cups sunflower oil
2 cups dry white wine
6 heaped Tbsp coarse salt

Serves 12–16

Lamb

1 x 20 kg lean lamb

Baste

6 cups No. 1 Greek-style marinade (page 12), or No. 22 Orange and herb marinade (page 17) are recommended

It is not practical to marinate a lamb in domestic circumstances and, if the lamb is of the best quality, it should not be necessary provided that the lamb is basted frequently.

Serves 20–30

Argentinean spit-roast baste

6 black peppercorns
2 blades of mace or ½ tsp grated nutmeg
1 whole clove
2 whole allspice or ½ tsp ground allspice
1 bay leaf
1 onion, coarsely chopped
4 cloves garlic
⅓ cup dry white wine
2 Tbsp white vinegar
2 tsp Worcestershire sauce
2 Tbsp tomato purée
½ cup coarse salt

Place all the ingredients in a 750 ml screwtop jar, fill halfway with boiling water, stir and allow to cool slightly. Screw on the top, shake vigorously, remove the top and fill with tap water. Leave to stand for 24 hours. Perforate the top using a spike or metal skewer. Sprinkle the baste over the meat frequently during cooking. This baste can be used for lamb or beef. If used as a marinade, only use 1 cup of water.

When serving or cooking pork, most fruits, including papaw, oranges, apricots, prunes, plums, apples, kiwi fruit, pineapple and peaches, will complement the meat.

Braai buddy

RECIPE INDEX

Bastes 28
  Apple and chilli 30
  Basic mix 30
  BBQ chicken 30
  Beef, roast 31
  Creamy herb 31
  Lamb, leg of 31
  Lemon butter 31
  Portuguese red pepper paste 31
  Spare rib 30

Beef
  Ginger stir-fry 91
  Marinade 21, 22
  Marrow bones, grilled 86
  Potjiekos 73
  Roast, baste for 31
  Skewers, Portuguese 82

Burgers 46
  Accompaniments 51
  Basic burger mix 47
  BBQ 49
  Boere or sausage 49
  Caribbean 50
  Cheese-stuffed 48
  Chilli 48
  Condiments and sauces 51
  Country 49
  Curry 50
  Deluxe burger mix 47
  Garlic 48
  Herb 48
  Lamb 50
  Lemon-tarragon 49
  Mediterranean 48
  Mustard 49
  Onion 49
  Peri-peri 50
  Pork 49
  Ranch 49
  Sosatie 50
  Spicy 48
  Teriyaki 50

Chicken
  BBQ, baste for 30
  Kebabs 59
  Livers, Portuguese 82
  Marinade 17, 21
  Orange stir-fry 89
  Peri-peri 83
  Pineapple kebabs 59
  Potjiekos
    à la king 71
    De Waal's 72
    Garlic 70
    Ginger 71
    Liver 70
  Skottel-fried 90
  Stir-fry 89
  Thai 84

Dry rubs 24
  Basic 27
  Cajun spice mix 26
  Dry fish masala 27
  Dry marinade 27
  Tandoori mix 26

Favourite recipes 82
  Beef marrow bones, grilled 86
  Beef skewers (espatadas), Portuguese 82
  Chicken livers, Portuguese 82
  Chicken peri-peri, Lourenzo Marques 83
  Chicken peri-peri, Mozambique 83
  Chicken, Thai 84
  Eisbein, grilled 85
  Lamb breast, glazed 86
  Lamb, Mediterranean rack 85
  Lamb, Middle Eastern leg 87
  Lamb souvlaki 87
  Lamb steaks 86
  Spare ribs 84
  Venison, grilled leg 85

Fish and seafood 78
  Angelfish (Portuguese-style), grilled 80
  Calamari (Italian-style), marinated 79
  Marinade 16, 18, 19
  Masala 18
  Mussel potjiekos 76
  Pickled fish, Cape 81
  Pickled fish, Greek 81
  Sardines, grilled 79
  Snoek, Kaapse 79
  Swordfish (Turkish-style), grilled skewered 80

Glazes 32
  Apple cider 35
  Apricot 34
  Coffee 35
  Lemon 34
  Maple syrup 34
  Pineapple 34
  Plum 35
  Raisin 35

Kebabs 52
  Beef, tropical 56
  Chicken 59
  Chicken and pineapple 59
  Kebab banquet 53
  Lamb 57
  Lamb's kidney and liver 56
  Meat, mixed 57
  Moroccan 55
  Pork 55
  Shish kebabs 54
  Spanish 58
  Venison 58

Lamb
  Baste 31
  Breast, glazed 86
  Burger 50
  Kebabs 57
    Kidney and liver 56
  Leg, Middle Eastern 87
  Marinade 15, 21, 22
  Potjiekos
    Clanwilliam 72
    Curry 77
    Mediterranean 74
    Pumpkin 76
    Tomato 67
    Waterblommetjie 69
  Rack, Mediterranean 85

Shish kebabs 54
Souvlaki 87
Spit-roast 94
Steaks 86

Marinades 8
Apple 19
Apricot and onion 19
BBQ, basic 14
Beef flat rib 22
Beef or lamb 21
Beer 13
Calamari (Chinese) 19
Calamari (Italian) 19
Caribbean 14
Chicken or pork 21
Chicken (savoury) 17
Cola 14
Fajitas 18
Fish 16
Fish masala 18
Greek-style 12
Herb mix, poultry 23
Herb mix, meat 23
Honey 13
Kebabs, Spanish 20
Kidney and liver 15
Lamb, butterflied
  shoulder 22
Lamb chops 21
Lamb, whole cuts
  (herb) 21
Lemon and tarragon 13
Lime 17
Martini 20
Moroccan 15
Mustard and herb 20
Orange and herb 17
Peri-peri 12
Peri-peri oil 18
Pork chops 23

Pork or lamb 21
Pork, whole cuts 22
Port 23
Red wine 13
Saratoga chops 22
Satay 16
Seafood 16
Shish kebabs 15
Sosaties 15
Spring onion and
  soy 17
Steaks (soy and
  ginger) 23
Swordfish,
  Portuguese 18
Tandoori 12
Teriyaki 14
Yoghurt 20
Yoghurt or buttermilk 16

Mutton
Cabbage potjiekos 75
Potjiekos 66

Pork
Burger 49
Kebabs 55
Marinade 21, 22, 23
Potjiekos
  Lentil 67
  Pineapple 75
Sausage 62
Stir-fry, Chinese 88
Spit-roast 94

Poultry see Chicken
Potjiekos 64
Chicken à la king 71
Chicken and garlic 70
Chicken and ginger 71
Chicken, De Waal's 72
Chicken liver 70
Chilli con carne 68

Clanwilliam 72
Eastern beef 73
Green bean curry 77
Jambalaya 68
Lamb and tomato 67
Lamb curry 77
Mediterranean
  lamb 74
Mussel 76
Mutton 66
Mutton and cabbage 75
Oxtail 66
Pork and lentil 67
Pork and pineapple 75
Portuguese beef 73
Pumpkin 76
Steak and stout 69
Waterblommetjie 69

Sauces 36
Apple 43
BBQ, American 37
BBQ, basic 35, 36
BBQ, traditional 37
Chilli oil 45
Chilli paste, green
  Thai 45
Chilli paste, Mexican 44
Garlic butter 43
Garlic mayonnaise 40
Green pepper and
  tomato relish 40
Mint 43
Monkey gland 40
Mushroom 42
Mustard 43
Peri-peri 42
Pesto 40
Port 42
Remoulade 38
Sweet-and-sour 38, 39

Tomato 41
Tomato relish, spicy 38
Tomatoes and red
  peppers, Italian 41
Worcestershire
  sauce 38

Sausages 60
Bockwurst 63
Boerewors 61
Boerewors, the best
  ever 61
Bratwurst, grilled 61
Burger 49
Karoo 62
Mediterranean fry 88
Pork 62

Seafood see Fish and
  seafood

Skottel cooking 88
Beef and ginger
  stir-fry 91
Breakfast, the drinking
  man's 91
Chicken and orange
  stir fry 89
Chicken pieces, skottel
  fried 90
Chicken stir-fry 89
Chops, Skottel-fried 90
Pork stir-fry, Chinese 88
Sausage fry,
  Mediterranean 88
Vegetable stir-fry 90

Spit-roasting 92
Argentinean baste 94
Lamb 94
Pork 94

Venison
Grilled leg 85
Kebabs 58